TAKE ONE CAN

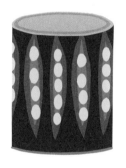

TAKE ONE CAN

80 DELICIOUS MEALS
FROM THE CUPBOARD

Lola Milne

Photography by Lizzie Mayson

Kyle Books

An Hachette UK Company
www.hachette.co.uk

This edition published in 2020.
First published in Great Britain in 2020 by
Kyle Books, an imprint of Kyle Cathie Ltd
Carmelite House, 50 Victoria Embankment,
London, EC4Y 0DZ
www.kylebooks.com

ISBN: 9780 85783 718 9

Distributed in the US by Hachette Book Group,
1290 Avenue of the Americas, 4th and 5th Floors,
New York, NY 10104

Distributed in Canada by Canadian Manda Group,
664 Annette St., Toronto, Ontario, Canada M6S 2C8

Publisher: Joanna Copestick
Editorial Director: Judith Hannam
Editor: Isabel Gonzalez-Prendergast
Americanizer: Lee Faber
Photographer: Lizzie Mayson
Designer: Louise Leffler
Food stylist: Lola Milne
Prop stylist: Louie Waller
Illustrator: We are Out of Office
Production: Emily Noto

A Cataloguing in Publication record for this title is
available from the British Library.

10 9 8 7 6 5 4 3 2 1

Printed and bound in China

CONTENTS

INTRODUCTION

The cupboard is a wondrous thing; I am always dipping in, whether to begin a meal, to embellish one, or to create an entire dish. Within the cupboard you will always find the humble can — cheap, nutritious, and long lasting. This book showcases these versatile creatures and gives you all sorts of new ideas on how to use them.

You can pick up a can of tomatoes or tuna almost anywhere. The can is universal, affordable, and accessible. No need for snobbery: the can is an undervalued resource. Every recipe in this book has something canned at its core; from black beans to sardines or pears, each is the springboard for a quick, easy, and delicious meal. Canned food shouldn't be bland or dull; I hope to show you how to create new and exciting dishes from familiar canned foods, and introduce you to some lesser-used canned friends-to-be.

Take One Can is for people who want to inject some oomph into their Wednesday dinner, reinvent those cupboard essentials, and be introduced to some more unfamiliar ingredients that are just sitting on the shelf waiting to be discovered. Whether you're after a restorative breakfast or a yummy dessert, you'll find perfect recipes here all (pretty much) from the comfort of the canned aisle.

The bulk of the ingredients used in support of the mighty can are also from the cupboard, meaning each recipe can be made without a shopping list as long as your arm; many recipes in the book have 10 ingredients or less. Cupboard staples are topped up with fresh ingredients that can easily be found in most stores.

You'll notice that there isn't any meat in this book. I am no vegetarian, but I do see the importance of eating less meat for both environmental and health reasons. It has been great to get creative with vegetables, pulses, and fish, and not look to meat to be the center of any dish. Of course, meat could be added to many of the dishes in this book, but I think they hold their own as they are. Hopefully you'll agree.

The chapters have been arranged to showcase the range of cans available, beginning with the staple that is beans and pulses. I am a true worshiper of the pulse. Tomatoes and vegetables come next, which play a central role in countless dishes. The book then goes on to the fish section, where I think you will be surprised at the range of delicious and affordable dishes you can make. The fruit and sweet cans chapter was heavily inspired by summers spent plodding about on my parent's community garden, helping them harvest, then watching them cooking and preserving their hauls of berries, pears, and peaches. This chapter showcases the amazing canned fruit you can get all year around, as well as things to make from cupboard staples, like coconut milk. The final chapter provides you with a few tasty accompaniments to eat alongside your meal, all very simple and made using ingredients that are predominantly from your cupboard.

A couple of practical bits: the oven temperatures are written for convection ovens; to convert to non-fan, simply add 25°F. There are a few recipes that either require or benefit from a stick blender or electric beaters; they are both great, small, and cheap pieces of kit to have in your kitchen.

I hope this book helps you see how accessible, achievable — and often even joyous — cooking can be and to realize that it doesn't always need to be about fresh or expensive ingredients. My wish for this book is that it leads you to the conclusion that the can is a wondrous thing.

BEANS & PULSES

SPICED CANNELLINI BEANS ON TOAST

Who doesn't love baked beans? These are a homemade alternative: sweet, spicy, and warming. Top with a fried egg for a classic breakfast.

SERVES 2

1 tablespoon olive oil

1 garlic clove, minced

¼ teaspoon red pepper flakes

pinch of paprika

14oz can plum tomatoes

2 teaspoons Worcestershire sauce

1 teaspoon soft brown sugar

2 teaspoons cider vinegar

15oz can cannellini beans, drained and rinsed

salt and freshly ground black pepper

2 slices of bread

Heat the olive oil in a large frying pan over medium-low heat. Once warm, add the garlic, fry until starting to turn golden, then add the spices, and cook for an additional 30 seconds. Tip in the plum tomatoes, Worcestershire sauce, sugar, vinegar, and cannellini beans. Season, bring to a boil, then simmer on a medium–high heat for 15–20 minutes until slightly thickened.

Toast your bread, and serve piled high with the beans, topped with a fried egg, if you like.

GREEN LENTIL FRITTERS

These are perfect for a lazy weekend brunch, topped with a fried egg. Beets can be swapped for parsnips or carrots (or pretty much any root veg).

SERVES 2 (ABOUT 6–8 FRITTERS)

14oz can green lentils, drained and rinsed

generous ½ cup all-purpose flour

1 egg, beaten

3 tablespoons chopped chives

1 teaspoon caraway seeds

1½ teaspoons paprika

1 garlic clove, minced

7oz/1 medium raw beet, peeled and coarsely grated

1–2 tablespoons flavorless oil (such as sunflower)

salt and freshly ground black pepper

TO SERVE

1 teaspoon harissa

2 tablespoons yogurt

Mix together the lentils, flour, egg, chives, caraway seeds, paprika, garlic, and beet, and then season.

Warm the oil in a large frying pan over medium heat. For each fritter, dollop in a heaping tablespoon of mixture, flatten slightly and fry until golden (about 4 minutes per side). If they start to color too soon, turn the heat down to low.

Meanwhile, mix the harissa into the yogurt.

Serve the fritters with a generous spoonful of the harissa yogurt.

GREEN LENTIL LASAGNA

I feel like vegetable lasagna has a bad reputation, and is unfairly sidelined. This lasagna is packed full of veg, and the creamy ricotta and spinach layer is a speedy and delicious alternative to a traditional béchamel sauce.

SERVES 6

2 tablespoons olive oil

2 red onions, minced

2 garlic cloves, peeled

3 bay leaves

28oz can chopped tomatoes

2 × 14oz cans green lentils, drained and rinsed

1lb fresh spinach

18oz ricotta cheese

pinch of ground nutmeg

12 lasagna sheets

jar of roasted red peppers, drained, rinsed, and opened out flat

scant cup grated Parmesan or Grana Padano cheese

salt and freshly ground black pepper

Preheat the oven to 350°F. In a large frying pan, heat the olive oil. Add the onions, garlic, and bay leaves, then sweat gently for 15 minutes. Fish out the garlic cloves, and add the tomatoes and lentils. Bring to a boil, then simmer on medium heat for 15 minutes. Turn off, and fish out the bay leaves.

To make the white layer of the lasagna, wilt the spinach in a saucepan, and then press into a strainer to get rid of as much water as possible. Tip into a bowl, and mix the spinach with the ricotta and nutmeg. Season and set aside.

To layer up the lasagna: spread a third of the tomato mixture into the base of an 8 × 12 inch baking dish. Top with a layer of pasta, and then a layer of the ricotta mixture, followed by a layer of the peppers. Repeat, ending with the final third of tomato mixture.

Cover the top with the grated cheese, then bake in the oven for 35–45 minutes until golden and bubbling. Leave to stand for 5–10 minutes before serving: it'll be easier to cut and handle.

LENTIL LINGUINE WITH CARAWAY CABBAGE

Inspired by delicious buttery cabbage and egg noodles I had in Budapest, this dish is a nod to the flavors of Eastern Europe: sweet and sharp, with a hint of caraway, balanced by the earthiness of lentils.

SERVES 2

1¾ tablespoons butter

1 large onion, finely sliced

¼ white cabbage, roughly sliced

1 teaspoon caraway seeds

pinch of superfine or granulated sugar

14oz can brown lentils, drained and rinsed

2 teaspoons white wine vinegar

7oz linguine (or spaghetti)

2 tablespoons sour cream (or crème fraîche or Greek yogurt), plus extra to serve

salt and freshly ground black pepper

Start by melting the butter gently over medium-low heat in your largest and deepest frying pan with a lid. When it starts to foam, add the onion, cabbage, and caraway seeds, season, and then add the sugar, turn the heat to low, and fry, covered, for 30 minutes. Check on it now and then to make sure it's not drying out or sticking.

Take the lid off, turn the heat up to medium, and continue to cook until the cabbage and onion are starting to turn golden. This should take about 10–15 minutes. Next, add your lentils and vinegar to the pan, and continue to cook for 5 minutes.

Boil the pasta in salted water according to package instructions, or until tender, reserve a mug of the cooking water, then drain.

Add the pasta to the frying pan, and mix, adding enough of the reserved cooking water to make the sauce coat the pasta. Stir in the sour cream, and remove from the heat.

Serve with an extra spoonful of sour cream, and some black pepper.

CHICKPEAS, SPICED CARROTS, & TAHINI

I like eating this mounded on buttery, herby couscous, or alongside a couple of sausages.

SERVES 2

3 carrots, sliced into thick chunks

1½ tablespoons olive oil

1 teaspoon ground cumin

pinch of ground cinnamon

pinch of red pepper flakes

2 garlic cloves, minced

15oz can chickpeas (garbanzo beans), drained and rinsed

1 tablespoon chopped dill

salt and freshly ground black pepper

FOR THE DRESSING

1½ tablespoons olive oil

1 tablespoon tahini

3 tablespoons plain yogurt

juice of 1 lemon

Preheat the oven to 350°F. In a roasting pan, toss the carrots with the olive oil, all the spices, and two-thirds of the garlic. Season and roast in the oven for 15 minutes, until starting to go a vibrant golden orange color. At this point, mix in the chickpeas, and continue to roast for an additional 10 minutes.

Meanwhile, make the dressing. Stir together the olive oil and reserved garlic, along with the tahini, yogurt, and lemon juice until smooth, then season and set aside until required.

To serve, pile the chickpeas and carrots onto a platter, drizzle with the dressing, and sprinkle over the dill.

CANNELLINI BEAN SOUP

This recipe plays on the classic combo of rosemary and garlic. The soft, creamy beans with the warmth of garlic, and the heady pine flavor of rosemary work beautifully together. Use organic cannellini beans if possible: they taste better, as does their liquid.

SERVES 4

3 tablespoons olive oil

1 large onion, minced

1 celery stalk, finely chopped

4 sprigs of rosemary, leaves chopped

4 garlic cloves, sliced

pinch of red pepper flakes

2 ×14oz cans cannellini beans (not drained)

½ teaspoon white wine vinegar

salt and freshly ground black pepper

TO SERVE

1 quantity Bread Crumb Topping (page 155) with optional almonds

grated Parmesan cheese (optional)

Heat the olive oil in a large saucepan over medium-low heat, tip in the onion and celery, along with a pinch of salt, and then sweat gently for 10 minutes, stirring often. Add the rosemary, garlic, and red pepper flakes, then cook for a few more minutes.

Tip in the cannellini beans along with their liquid, then fill the empty can with water, and add this to the pan. Season, bring to a boil, and then simmer over medium heat for 15 minutes.

Stir through the vinegar, then ladle the soup into bowls, and top with a generous sprinkling of the bread crumb mixture and grated Parmesan.

CHICKPEA & SQUASH TAGINE

This dish is perfect for autumnal days, where you're feeling in need of a dose of warming spices. If you fancy, try using a mixture of root vegetables, or chuck in some eggplant, too.

SERVES 4

2 tablespoons olive oil

2 red onions, thinly sliced

½ teaspoon ground cinnamon

1 teaspoon ground ginger

1 teaspoon ground coriander

1 teaspoon sweet paprika

½ teaspoon ground cumin

2 bay leaves

½ butternut squash, peeled, seeded, and cut into small chunks

2 × 14oz cans chickpeas (garbanzo beans) (not drained)

14oz can plum tomatoes

¼ cup roughly chopped dried apricots

salt and freshly ground black pepper

TO SERVE

couscous or rice

chopped cilantro (optional)

Heat the olive oil in a large saucepan, add the onions, and sweat gently for 10–15 minutes, until turning translucent and tinged golden.

At this point, add all the spices and bay leaves to the onion mixture. Cook for a minute, then add the squash. Toss it in the spices to coat, tip in the chickpeas (along with their liquid), tomatoes, and apricots. Top up the pan with enough water to just cover the vegetables, then season. Bring to a boil, then simmer over low heat for 55–65 minutes until the sauce has thickened a little, and the vegetables are tender. Give it a stir now and then to check nothing is sticking, and that it hasn't dried out. When serving, carefully remove the bay leaves.

Serve on piles of couscous or rice with a sprinkling of chopped cilantro, if you like.

JACKFRUIT & KIDNEY BEAN CHILI

When jackfruit is cooked, weirdly it shreds just like pulled pork, which gives this chili a more substantial meatiness. You want to buy young "green" jackfruit in water for this recipe. Perfect served as part of a Mexican-style feast.

SERVES 4

2 tablespoons olive oil

2 onions, minced

2 garlic cloves, minced

1 bay leaf

1 teaspoon ground cumin

1 teaspoon ground cinnamon

1½ teaspoons dried red pepper flakes or chili powder (ancho or chipotle)

28oz can chopped tomatoes

14oz can kidney beans, drained and rinsed

14oz can black beans (not drained)

14oz can jackfruit, drained and rinsed

scant ½ cup strong brewed coffee

1 teaspoon dried oregano

salt and freshly ground black pepper

Heat the oil in a large saucepan over medium heat, add the onions, then reduce the heat to low, and sweat for 15–20 minutes until soft.

Add the garlic, bay leaf, cumin, cinnamon, and red pepper flakes, and sweat for an additional 2–3 minutes. Next, add the tomatoes, kidney and black beans, plus the black bean liquid, jackfruit, coffee, and oregano, then season. Bring to a boil, and then turn down the heat and simmer gently for 45–50 minutes until thickened, and the jackfruit is tender. Finally, break up the jackfruit with a wooden spoon until it resembles pulled pork in texture.

Try serving it with rice, or spooned onto corn tortillas with sour cream, guacamole, jalapeños, and a cheeky bit of grated Cheddar cheese.

Tip: Make a day ahead to allow the flavors to mingle more; it's made better by waiting.

GREEK LIMA BEANS

Perfect on toast and covered in feta or topped with a poached egg.

SERVES 2

2 tablespoons olive oil

1 onion, minced

2 garlic cloves, sliced

½ teaspoon ground cinnamon

½ teaspoon chili flakes (ancho or chipotle)

15oz can lima beans, drained and rinsed

14oz can chopped tomatoes

1 teaspoon dried oregano

1 tablespoon chopped fresh dill

salt and freshly ground black pepper

Heat the olive oil in a frying pan over medium-low heat, add the onion, turn to low, and gently soften for 10–15 minutes. Add the garlic, cinnamon, and chili flakes, and continue to fry for a few minutes.

Add the lima beans, tomatoes, and oregano, then season. Bring to a boil, and then simmer gently for 15–20 minutes until thickened a little.

Serve the beans sprinkled with the dill.

LIMA BEAN, LENTIL, & CHICKPEA STEW

Cooking the onions long and slow creates an amazing depth of flavor.

SERVES 4

2 tablespoons olive oil, plus extra for drizzling

2 onions, minced

2 garlic cloves, sliced

2 bay leaves

1½ teaspoons dried mint

1 teaspoon ground turmeric

15oz can lima beans, drained and rinsed

14oz can lentils, drained and rinsed

14oz can chickpeas, drained and rinsed

2 cups vegetable stock

7oz fresh spinach

salt and freshly ground black pepper

In a large saucepan, heat the olive oil over low heat. Sweat the onions gently with a pinch of salt until very soft and tinged golden (this will take 30–40 minutes). Then add the garlic, bay leaves, mint, and turmeric. Continue to cook for a few minutes until the garlic has softened.

Tip in the lima beans, lentils, and chickpeas along with the stock. Bring to a boil, then turn up to medium-low heat and cook for 20–25 minutes. Add the spinach, and allow it to wilt, stirring to incorporate it, then season.

To serve, ladle into bowls and top with an extra drizzle of olive oil. Watch out for the bay leaves when eating.

CABBAGE WITH ANCHOVIES & LENTILS

The sweetness of roasted cabbage is a perfect partner to salty anchovies and earthy lentils.

SERVES 2 AS A LIGHT MEAL OR 4 AS A SIDE

1 sweetheart (sometimes called pointed or hispi) cabbage

2 tablespoons olive oil

6 canned anchovy fillets, drained and finely chopped

3 garlic cloves, sliced

14oz can beluga lentils, drained and rinsed

juice of ½ lemon

2 shallots, finely sliced

handful of parsley, roughly chopped

salt and freshly ground black pepper

Preheat the oven to 400°F. Cut the cabbage into about eight wedges, and add to a large roasting pan.

In a small frying pan, gently heat the olive oil and anchovies, until the anchovies have begun to break down. Add the garlic, fry for about 2–3 minutes, then pour this fragrant oil over the cabbage, and season (go easy on the salt, as anchovies are really salty). Toss to combine, add 2 tablespoons of water, then roast for 10–20 minutes until the cabbage is tender and crisp at the edges.

Once the cabbage is cooked, add the lentils to the pan, and then roast for an additional 2–3 minutes just to warm through.

Meanwhile, put the lemon juice and shallots into a bowl and set aside.

Once the cabbage and lentils are ready, stir through the shallots and parsley. Serve with hunks of bread or on garlic-rubbed toast.

LEEKS, FLAGEOLET BEANS, & BLUE CHEESE

This dish works well as part of a spread of salads, as a side for fish or meat, or on its own served over some cheesy, soft polenta. Roquefort, Stilton, or Gorgonzola would all work.

SERVES 2–3 AS A SIDE

FOR THE DRESSING

1 shallot, minced

1 tablespoon white wine vinegar

1 tablespoon olive oil

½ teaspoon grainy mustard

1 tablespoon butter

½ tablespoon olive oil

3 large leeks, ends trimmed, cut into thirds horizontally, and then cut in half vertically

1¼ cups vegetable stock

14oz can flageolet beans, drained and rinsed

3oz blue cheese

salt and freshly ground black pepper

Put the shallot and vinegar in a bowl or cup and set aside.

In a deep frying pan, melt the butter with the olive oil, then add the leek slices, and brown a little all over. Ensure all the leeks are in a single layer on the base of the pan, and then pour in enough stock to come halfway up the leeks (you don't need to use all of the stock). Bring to a boil, and then simmer over medium-low heat for 5–10 minutes, until the stock has evaporated, and the leeks are tender. Add the flageolet beans, and cook for another 2–3 minutes just to warm them.

Once the leeks are cooked, and the beans warm, finish making the dressing: add the mustard and olive oil to the shallot and vinegar mixture, season, and whisk to combine.

Tip the leeks and flageolet beans onto a large plate or platter, drizzle over the dressing, and dot with little pieces of blue cheese.

POTATO & GREAT NORTHERN BEAN HASH

This dish can be mixed up with different leftovers. Swap beets for other root veg, throw in cooked greens, or add chorizo, bacon, or sausages (if you're that way inclined).

SERVES 4

4 tablespoons butter

1 onion, coarsely chopped

2 medium boiled potatoes, peeled and coarsely chopped

1 large cooked beet, coarsely chopped

15½oz can great northern beans, drained and rinsed

4 heaping tablespoons sauerkraut, plus extra to serve

4 eggs

salt and freshly ground black pepper

In a large frying pan, melt half of the butter. Meanwhile, in a bowl, mix the onion, potatoes, beets, great northern beans, and sauerkraut, then season. Tip into the frying pan, press down firmly and cook over medium-low heat for 20 minutes, until a nice crust forms on the base. Stir and break up the mixture a bit to distribute the crust throughout, then press down again to cook for an additional 20 minutes. Repeat once more, this time cooking for 15 minutes over low heat.

When you're almost ready to serve, melt the remaining butter in another frying pan. When it starts to foam, crack in the eggs, season, and fry until the whites have set, and the undersides have started to crisp up.

Spoon the hash onto plates, and top each portion with a fried egg and extra sauerkraut.

ROASTED CHICKPEAS & SQUASH PASTA

The sweetness and softness of squash works brilliantly with the crisp, mild nuttiness of the chickpeas, all wrapped in gloriously warming spices, and served with tart yogurt, and a lemony bread crumb crunch.

SERVES 2 GENEROUSLY

1 small butternut squash or pumpkin, peeled, seeded, and chopped into walnut-sized chunks

½ teaspoon red pepper flakes

½ teaspoon fennel seeds

½ teaspoon cumin seeds

generous pinch of ground cinnamon

3 garlic cloves, minced

2 tablespoons olive oil

14oz can chickpeas (garbanzo beans), drained and rinsed

7oz angel hair/vermicelli pasta

2 tablespoons plain yogurt

2 tablespoons chopped parsley

salt and freshly ground black pepper

½ quantity Bread Crumb Topping with optional lemon zest, to serve (page 155)

Preheat your oven to 350°F.

In a large roasting pan, toss together the squash, red pepper flakes, fennel and cumin seeds, cinnamon, garlic, and oil, then season, and roast for 20 minutes, or until the squash is starting to turn golden and soft, but still holding its shape.

Toss the chickpeas through, and roast in the oven for an additional 10 minutes.

Meanwhile, boil the pasta in salted water according to package instructions, or until tender, reserve a mug of the cooking water, then drain.

Using a potato masher, roughly crush about half the butternut squash and chickpeas. Add the pasta, yogurt, parsley, and enough of the reserved cooking water to the pan to coat the pasta in the sauce. Adjust the seasoning, top with the bread crumb mixture, and serve.

COMFORTING BLACK BEANS

These beans are earthy, salty, and smoky. So simple and so delicious. Enjoyed with rice, wrapped in a burrito, or fried in a quesadilla, these beans always fill the bill.

SERVES 4

1 tablespoon olive oil

1 large onion, minced

2 garlic cloves, sliced

1 bay leaf

2 teaspoons chili flakes or powder (ancho or chipotle)

pinch of ground cinnamon

½ teaspoon ground cumin

2 carrots, cut into rounds

2 × 15¼oz cans black beans (not drained)

1¼ cups vegetable stock

salt and freshly ground black pepper

Begin by heating the olive oil in a large frying pan. Add the onion and soften gently for 10 minutes. Then add the garlic, bay leaf, chili flakes or powder, cinnamon, cumin, and carrots and cook for an additional 2–3 minutes. Tip in the black beans and stock. Bring to a boil, and cook over medium heat for about 20–25 minutes, until the mixture has thickened a little, then season.

Pile into bowls, and serve with rice or a dollop of sour cream, and some cilantro, if you like.

ROASTED ZUCCHINI & CANNELLINI BEAN DIP

This is quite like hummus and it's delicious eaten warm or cold with soft flatbreads or veg crudités. Za'atar is magic — try sprinkling it on broiled fish, roasted veggies or salads.

SERVES 4

4 zucchini, sliced into chunky rounds

4 tablespoons olive oil, plus extra for drizzling

juice of ½ lemon

2 garlic cloves, crushed

2 tablespoons tahini

14oz can cannellini beans, drained and rinsed

1 teaspoon za'atar spice mix

salt and freshly ground black pepper

Preheat the oven to 425°F.

Spread the zucchini over two baking sheets, drizzle with half the olive oil, season, and then roast for 20–25 minutes until golden and tender. The undersides seem to brown much more quickly, so check after about 10–15 minutes and flip if necessary.

Blend two-thirds of the roasted zucchini with the remaining olive oil and the lemon juice, garlic, tahini, and cannellini beans until smooth, then season. Tip into a bowl and top with the remaining zucchini. Sprinkle over the za'atar, and drizzle with extra olive oil.

LIMA BEAN, BELL PEPPER, & WALNUT SALAD

This is a great dish to make ahead and take for lunch with couscous. If you don't have lima beans, you can use cannellini or great northern beans, instead.

SERVES 2 GENEROUSLY

FOR THE DRESSING

3 red, orange, or yellow bell peppers

¾ cup walnut halves

large bunch of parsley, minced

1 garlic clove, minced

¹/₃ cup olive oil

1 tablespoon sherry vinegar

7oz cherry tomatoes, halved

15oz can lima beans, drained and rinsed

1 small red onion, sliced as finely as possible

2 tablespoons capers, drained and roughly chopped

salt and freshly ground black pepper

Preheat the oven to 425°F.

Put the whole peppers on a baking sheet, and roast for 30–35 minutes until well blackened, adding the walnuts to the sheet for the final 3 minutes of roasting, until a shade darker, and smelling fragrant.

Once the peppers are cooked, tip into a bowl and cover with plastic wrap (this will make peeling much easier), and set the walnuts aside to cool.

When the peppers are cool enough to handle, peel, seed, and finely chop them. Once the walnuts are cool, finely chop.

In a large bowl, make the dressing: mix the chopped peppers and walnuts with the parsley, garlic, oil and vinegar, then season. Toss with the tomatoes, lima beans, red onion and capers. Serve on couscous or with garlic-rubbed toast.

CHICKPEA & ONION BHAJIS

These crispy treats are sweet and spicy. Ensure you crush all the chickpeas a little; if you don't, they tend to explode when deep-fried. Always be really careful when deep-frying.

MAKES ABOUT 10

¾ cup all-purpose flour

scant ½ cup plain yogurt

2 teaspoons mild curry powder

1 teaspoon ground cumin

1 teaspoon chili powder

14oz can chickpeas (garbanzo beans), drained, rinsed, and lightly crushed

2 large onions, thinly sliced

2 quarts sunflower oil, for frying

salt and freshly ground black pepper

Tip: Try adding 15 thinly sliced curry leaves to the bhaji mixture.

In a large bowl, beat the flour and yogurt together to make a smooth paste. Add the spices, chickpeas, and onions, then season.

Add the oil to a large saucepan (it should only come halfway up the side of the pan) and place over medium-high heat. Line a baking sheet with paper towels. Wait a few minutes, then test whether the oil is hot enough by dropping a small piece of batter in; if it is hot enough, it should sizzle immediately.

When the oil is hot enough, gently drop in heaping tablespoons of the mixture, using a second spoon to scrape it off the first. Fry each for 4–5 minutes, turning halfway through, until golden all over. Remove from the oil using a slotted spoon, and place on the paper-lined sheet to drain. Repeat until all the mixture is used up. Once finished, turn off the heat, and leave the oil to cool completely before cleaning up.

Serve the bhajis with Mango Chutney (page 151).

LENTIL, CHEESE, & ONION PUFF PIE

This pie is an appreciation of the cheese and onion pasties of my Devonshire childhood holidays, but this one has the addition of nutty lentils, sweet squash, and sneaks in a bit of tangy sauerkraut. Eat while it's hot, and the cheese is oozing.

SERVES 6

½ butternut squash, peeled, seeded, and cut into chunks

1 tablespoon olive oil

½ teaspoon red pepper flakes

½ teaspoon nigella seeds

2 tablespoons butter

2 large onions, finely sliced

7fl oz dry hard cider

3 tablespoons all-purpose flour

7fl oz vegetable stock

14oz can beluga lentils, drained and rinsed (or you can use cooked lentils in a pouch)

9oz aged Cheddar cheese, grated

1 generous cup sauerkraut

ready-rolled puff pastry sheet, about 11½oz

1 egg, beaten

salt and freshly ground black pepper

Preheat the oven to 350°F. You'll need a ceramic or metal dish roughly 8 × 12 inches (or a 9–10-inch circular dish).

Toss the squash with the oil, pepper flakes and nigella seeds, tip onto a baking sheet, and roast for 20 minutes or until golden and soft, but still holding its shape. Set aside.

Meanwhile, melt the butter in a large frying pan, add the onions and a pinch of salt, then fry over low heat for 20 minutes, until soft and tinged golden.

Add the cider, bring to a boil, then rapidly simmer for 2 minutes. Next, add the flour, and stir to combine, then simmer for another 2 minutes. Pour in the stock, and boil for a few minutes until thickened. Turn off the heat, and add the lentils, cheese, squash mixture and sauerkraut, then season.

Add the filling to your dish, and lay the pastry sheet over the top. Press onto the dish edge, trim away any excess, then poke a couple of holes in the pastry lid with a knife, and brush with the beaten egg. Place on a baking sheet, and bake in the oven for 35–40 minutes, until well-puffed and bubbling.

Eat (almost) immediately, while the filling is still fondue-like.

TOMATOES & VEGETABLES

CHERRY TOMATO TOASTS

These are a quick, fresh fix, perfect for brunch or lunch. The delicate creaminess of the ricotta is delicious with the tomatoes and punchy green sauce.

SERVES 2

14oz can cherry tomatoes

2 slices of bread

3oz ricotta cheese

salt and freshly ground black pepper

FOR THE GREEN SAUCE

2 tablespoons olive oil

1 garlic clove, minced

a handful of basil, leaves picked and finely chopped

3 sprigs of mint, leaves picked and finely choppedz

$^1/_3$ cup grated Parmesan cheese

1 teaspoon white wine or cider vinegar

Preheat the broiler to high.

Tip the cherry tomatoes onto a baking sheet and broil for 5–10 minutes until starting to blister.

Meanwhile, combine the olive oil with the garlic, herbs, Parmesan, and vinegar, season, and set aside. Toast the bread, then pop a slice on each plate. Top with the broiled tomatoes and ricotta, spoon over the green sauce and enjoy.

SPICED TOMATO & LENTIL SOUP

Lentil soup has always been a meal of comfort for me; my mom often makes it with her homemade chicken stock, slightly different every time, but it always makes me feel cosy and nourished. It is such an easy and satisfying dish; perfect for a chilly evening.

SERVES 6

1½ tablespoons olive oil, plus extra to drizzle

1 onion, minced

3 garlic cloves, minced

½–1 teaspoon red pepper flakes

2 teaspoons ground cumin

2 teaspoons Thai 7 spice seasoning, or Baharat (or a pinch each of ground cinnamon, cumin, cloves, and nutmeg)

2 cups dried split red lentils

14oz can chopped tomatoes

2 bay leaves

juice of 1 lemon

salt and freshly ground black pepper

Warm the oil in a large saucepan over medium-low heat, add the onion, and cook slowly for about 10–15 minutes until softened. If it begins to brown, turn the heat down. Add the garlic, red pepper flakes, cumin, and spice mix, and fry for a couple of minutes. Add the lentils, tomatoes, bay leaves, and 2 quarts of water. Bring to a boil, and then simmer gently until the lentils have swelled, and are soft: this should take 25–30 minutes.

When the lentils are tender and breaking down, season, turn off the heat, and add the lemon juice. Spoon the soup (watching out for bay leaves) into bowls, and drizzle with a little olive oil.

Tip: Try topping the soup with roasted slices of zucchini or carrot: toss in olive oil, salt, pepper, and ground cumin, and bake in an oven preheated to 400°F for 15–20 minutes, or until golden and tender. Or try topping with a handful of chopped dill, parsley, or mint, and some crumbled feta cheese.

TURKISH SCRAMBLED EGGS

Digressing from the traditional scrambled eggs situation seemed slightly erroneous, but it was worth it: these are delicious. Serve with toasted pita bread for scooping.

SERVES 2

3 tablespoons olive oil

1 onion, minced

1 garlic clove, minced

2–3 fresh jalapeño peppers (or 1 green bell pepper), seeded, and finely chopped

½ teaspoon red pepper flakes

¼ teaspoon hot smoked paprika

½ teaspoon dried oregano

14oz can plum tomatoes, drained and quartered

4 eggs, lightly beaten

salt and freshly ground black pepper

Heat the oil in a frying pan over medium-low heat, tip in the onion and sweat for 5–10 minutes. Add the garlic, fresh jalapeños or bell pepper, red pepper flakes, paprika, and oregano and cook for another 5 minutes until the peppers start to soften. At this point, add the tomatoes, season, and then simmer for 15 minutes.

Turn the heat to low, then push the tomato mixture to the side of the frying pan. Add the eggs and gently stir until they are just cooked, then fold into the tomato mixture.

Serve with Quick Chapatis (see page 146) or with a generous dollop of yogurt.

TOMATOES, GARLIC, & GREEN BEANS

My Parisian cousin Sylvie is a great cook. A dish of hers that has stuck in my mind is her roast chicken on a bed of green beans and little tomatoes. This recipe is inspired by it. Serve alongside chicken, with fish, or simply with a hunk of bread or a slice of toast.

SERVES 2

7oz fine green beans, trimmed and cut in half

3 tablespoons olive oil

4 garlic cloves, sliced

28oz can plum tomatoes, drained

salt and freshly ground black pepper

bread, to serve

In a pan of boiling water, blanch the green beans for 3 minutes, then drain and set aside.

In a large frying pan, heat the olive oil, then add the garlic, and fry for a couple of minutes, until smelling fragrant and tinged golden. Add the drained tomatoes and green beans, then season. Bring to a boil, then reduce the heat, and simmer for 10 minutes, covered. Remove the lid, and simmer for an additional 10 minutes. Delicious hot or cold, and a hunk of bread to soak up all the juices is essential.

CORN CAKES WITH GREEN CHUTNEY

These sweet and mellow corn cakes go beautifully with the punchy, spicy, and tart chutney. This is a perfect brunch dish or light supper.

SERVES 3 GENEROUSLY

FOR THE CHUTNEY

about 2oz fresh cilantro, leaves picked

¾ oz fresh mint, leaves picked

1 garlic clove, roughly chopped

juice of ½ lemon

½ cup dried shredded coconut

1 green chile, finely chopped, and seeds left in if you like spice

salt and freshly ground black pepper

FOR THE CORN CAKES

14oz canned whole kernel corn (drained and half roughly blitzed)

2 eggs

¾ cup self-rising flour

2 teaspoons mild curry powder

1 small red onion, minced

1 tablespoon flavorless oil (such as sunflower)

To make the chutney, put the cilantro, mint, garlic, lemon juice, coconut, and chile with 2–3 tablespoons of water into a blender or food processor. Blitz until smooth, adding more water if needed (the final consistency should be like pesto). Season and set aside.

To make the corn cakes, in a large bowl, mix all the corn, the eggs, flour, curry powder and onion, then season.

Heat the oil in a large frying pan, then dollop in a heaping tablespoon of mixture for each cake. Flatten each slightly, and fry for 3–4 minutes per side until golden and crisp; you may need to do this in batches. Set each batch aside on a plate lined with paper towels while you cook the rest.

Serve the cakes with the bright green chutney, and garnish with a lemon wedge, if liked.

STICKY POTATOES WITH SPICY TOMATO SAUCE

Patatas bravas meets marinara sauce. The Marsala makes the potatoes sticky and sweet, but it can be swapped for anything similar you have at hand, such as stock or water.

SERVES 2

2 large baking potatoes, each cut into about 8 long wedges

2 garlic cloves

2 tablespoons olive oil

2 sprigs of rosemary

3½fl oz Marsala wine (or vegetable stock)

salt and freshly ground black pepper

FOR THE TOMATO SAUCE

1 tablespoon olive oil

1 garlic clove, sliced

1 teaspoon dried oregano

1 teaspoon red pepper flakes (use ½ teaspoon if they are extra hot)

14oz can chopped tomatoes

Preheat the oven to 400°F. On a large baking sheet, toss the potatoes with the garlic cloves (bashed with the skin on), the olive oil, and the rosemary, then season. Roast in the oven for 30 minutes. Add the Marsala (or stock), and then roast for an additional 15 minutes.

Meanwhile, make the sauce: heat the olive oil and add the sliced garlic, oregano, and red pepper flakes. Cook for 1 minute or so, then add the tomatoes. Season, bring to a boil, then cook for 15 minutes on medium-high heat. Blitz the sauce with a stick blender until smooth (or it can be left chunky, if preferred).

Remove the sticky potatoes from the oven, and serve immediately with the sauce.

Tip: Try beating 100g of feta cheese into 1 scant cup of sour cream: a cooling antidote to serve alongside the spicy tomato sauce.

BAMBOO SHOOT & EGGPLANT NOODLES

A deliciously creamy, spicy, and sweet bowl of salvation. The texture of eggplant when fried is a thing of beauty; buttery soft and silky. In this recipe, it's complemented by the crunch of bamboo shoots.

SERVES 2

FOR THE SATAY SAUCE

2 tablespoons crunchy peanut butter

1–2 tablespoons Chinese chili oil

2 garlic cloves, minced

2 tablespoons light soy sauce

1-inch piece of fresh ginger, peeled and grated (about 1½ tablespoons when grated)

1 tablespoon rice wine vinegar

FOR THE NOODLES

3½oz flat Thai-style rice noodles

2 tablespoons flavorless oil (such as sunflower)

1 eggplant, cut into 1-inch chunks

8oz can bamboo shoots, drained, and roughly sliced

3 scallions, sliced, whites and greens separated

Start by mixing everything for the sauce together along with ²/₃ cup warm water, then set aside.

Boil the noodles for 3 minutes, or according to the package instructions, then drain and refresh under cold water and set aside.

In a wok or large frying pan, heat the oil over medium-high heat, then add the eggplant and fry, stirring often, until tender and golden (about 5–10 minutes). Next, add the bamboo shoots and scallion whites, fry for another 2 minutes, then add the noodles and satay sauce, stirring to coat.

Pile onto plates, and top with the scallion greens.

TOMATO, LENTIL, & EGGPLANT RAGÙ

When I was growing up, my auntie Sophie often made a big pan of tomatoey lentils when we went around. This version is a nod to a traditional Italian meat ragù, but I have added eggplant instead, served with soft polenta & wilted greens.

SERVES 6

6 tablespoons olive oil

2 onions, minced

2 eggplants, cut into 1-inch cubes

2 garlic cloves, minced

½ teaspoon fennel seeds

2 bay leaves

pinch of red pepper flakes

7fl oz red wine

2 × 14oz cans beluga lentils, drained and rinsed

28oz can chopped tomatoes

salt and freshly ground black pepper

In a large frying pan, heat 2 tablespoons of the oil, add the onions, and soften over low heat for about 10–15 minutes.

Meanwhile, in another frying pan, heat the remaining oil, add the eggplant and a pinch of salt, then fry on high for 5–10 minutes, stirring often, until the eggplant cubes are golden. Set aside.

By this point, the onions should be soft and tinged golden. Add the garlic, fennel seeds, bay leaves, and red pepper flakes. Fry for another 2–3 minutes, then tip in the wine. Bring to a boil, and boil until it has reduced by two-thirds in volume (this shouldn't take more than 5 minutes). Last, but not least, add the lentils, tomatoes, and the browned eggplant cubes. Season, and reduce the heat, then simmer for 15–20 minutes until the sauce has thickened a little, and the eggplant is buttery soft.

This ragù is great with soft polenta, pasta, or served simply with a hunk of bread. Just before serving, fish out the bay leaves.

FLAGEOLET BEAN & ARTICHOKE GRATIN

If you don't eat fish, the anchovies can be left out. If you do eat fish, don't be tempted to leave them out anyway just because you think you don't like them; they bring a subtly salty depth to this rich and creamy dish.

SERVES 2

2 tablespoons butter

2 onions, chopped

3 garlic cloves, sliced

3 sprigs of rosemary, finely chopped

3 canned anchovy fillets, drained and finely chopped

1 cup soft, fresh bread crumbs

½ cup grated Parmesan cheese

14oz can flageolet beans, drained and rinsed

14oz can artichoke hearts in water, drained, rinsed, and torn in half

7fl oz heavy cream

salt and freshly ground black pepper

Tip: Experiment with adding a pinch of red pepper flakes when you're softening the onion.

Preheat the oven to 350°F. Melt the butter in a frying pan over medium-low heat. Once the butter is foaming, add the onions, garlic, rosemary, and anchovy fillets. Reduce the heat to low, and soften gently for 20–25 minutes until the onions are tender and turning golden.

Meanwhile, mix the bread crumbs with the cheese and set aside.

Once the onions have softened, add the beans and artichoke hearts, season, and heat through for 5–6 minutes, then add the cream. Bring the mixture almost to a boil, then tip into a baking dish, and top with the cheesy breadcrumbs. Bake for 25–30 minutes, until golden and bubbling. Serve with a hunk of crusty bread and some salad.

A CLASSIC TOMATO SOUP

I felt like it was a must to include this recipe in this book. Of course, a ready-made can of tomato soup has its place, but this soup has more depth and freshness, and it's almost as easy to make.

SERVES 2

2 tablespoons olive oil

1 onion, minced

1 celery stalk, finely chopped

1 carrot, diced

1 garlic clove, minced

1 teaspoon dried oregano

14oz can chopped tomatoes

pinch of sugar

½ teaspoon red wine vinegar

2 tablespoons crème fraîche

salt and freshly ground black pepper

a handful of basil, roughly chopped, to serve

In a large saucepan, heat the olive oil, then add the onion, celery, carrot, and garlic and soften gently for 10–15 minutes. Tip in the oregano, tomatoes, sugar, and 1¼ cups of water and season. Bring to a boil, then turn down the heat, and simmer for 20 minutes until thickened a little.

Either blitz smooth with a stick blender, or simply pass over with a potato masher for a chunkier soup. Stir in the vinegar.

Ladle into bowls, then swirl the crème fraîche into each and top with some basil.

INDIAN EGGS WITH TOMATOES

These eggs are simply flavored with sweetness from the tomatoes and coconut. This is a perfect breakfast served up with some chapatis and a good dollop of yogurt.

SERVES 2

1 tablespoon dried shredded coconut

1 tablespoon flavorless oil (such as sunflower)

½ teaspoon brown mustard seeds

1 shallot (or ½ onion), minced

1 green chile, seeded and finely chopped

10 fresh or dried curry leaves

¼ teaspoon ground turmeric

14oz can plum tomatoes, drained and rinsed

4 eggs, beaten and seasoned

salt and freshly ground black pepper

In a cup, cover the coconut with boiling water, then set aside.

Heat the oil in a medium frying pan over high heat, then add the mustard seeds. When they start to pop, which will be about 30 seconds, add the shallot and green chile, then reduce the heat to medium, and fry for 3–5 minutes until just starting to color.

Add the curry leaves and turmeric, then fry for another 30 seconds. Add the tomatoes and soaked coconut, along with its liquid, and roughly break each tomato into two or three pieces. Bring to a boil, and simmer for 5–10 minutes over medium heat until most of the liquid has evaporated. Season.

Scoop the tomato mixture into a bowl and set aside. Drip a little more oil into the pan, and turn the heat to medium-high. Tip in the eggs and allow them to set, pulling back the edges to allow any raw egg to fill the gaps. Cook until golden on the base and still damp on top. Dollop the tomato mixture evenly on top of the eggs. Cook for 30 seconds more, then fold in half, cut in two, and serve. Try serving with Quick Chapatis (see page 146), Mango Chutney (see page 151) and plain yogurt, if liked.

ARTICHOKE CARBONARA

Carbonara is such a quick supper. It is rich and creamy (without any cream), thanks to the egg yolks and mountains of cheese. Artichokes bring a slight citrus flavor that balances the richness of the sauce.

SERVES 2

2 tablespoons olive oil

2 onions, minced

1 large egg, plus 2 yolks

pinch of ground nutmeg

¾ cup finely grated Parmesan cheese, plus extra to serve

2 garlic cloves, sliced

14oz can artichoke hearts, drained, rinsed, and roughly torn

7oz spaghetti

salt and freshly ground black pepper

Heat the olive oil in a large frying pan over medium heat. Once hot, add the onion, turn the heat down, and sweat gently for 20 minutes.

Meanwhile, beat together the egg, extra yolks, nutmeg, and cheese, then season (be generous with the black pepper), and set aside.

Add the garlic to the pan and fry for 1 minute. Next, add the artichokes, cover with a lid, and heat gently while you cook the spaghetti.

Boil the spaghetti in a pan of salted water according to the package instructions, or until tender, scoop out a mug of cooking water, then drain.

Remove the frying pan from the heat, and immediately tip in the spaghetti. Toss in the sauce, and then pour in the egg and cheese mixture. Working quickly, toss the pasta in the mixture, taking care to not allow the eggs to sit on the base of the pan (they may scramble). Once the pasta is coated, add a little of the reserved cooking water, if needed, to create a glossy sauce.

Mound onto plates, and top with extra Parmesan and black pepper.

TOMATO, CHICKPEA, & OKRA MASALA

I love curry. I am a slight addict, and have recently come to the conclusion that most things are improved when curried.

SERVES 2

2½ tablespoons flavorless oil (such as sunflower)

1 teaspoon brown or black mustard seeds

1 teaspoon fenugreek seeds

1 large onion, thinly sliced

1-inch piece of fresh ginger, peeled and finely grated

3 garlic cloves, minced

3 teaspoons garam masala

14oz can chickpeas (garbanzo beans) (not drained)

14oz can plum tomatoes

18oz okra (ladies' fingers), trimmed, and sliced into 1¼ inch pieces

salt and freshly ground black pepper

Heat 1½ tablespoons of the oil in a deep frying pan. Once hot, add the mustard seeds, wait until they start to pop (about 30 seconds), and then add the fenugreek seeds. Shortly after, add the onion and a pinch of salt, turn the heat down, and sweat for 10–15 minutes until the onion is soft and turning golden.

Add the ginger, garlic, and 2 teaspoons of the garam masala and cook for an additional 3–4 minutes. Add the can of chickpeas, including their liquid, and the tomatoes. Season, and cook for 20 minutes, or until the tomatoes have broken down, and the curry has thickened a little.

Meanwhile, in a separate frying pan, heat the remaining oil and garam masala, then fry the okra pieces for 6–7 minutes, until nicely browned. Set aside.

Once the curry has thickened, add the okra, and cook for another 5–6 minutes. Serve steaming bowls of curry alongside Quick Chapatis (see page 146), yogurt, or Coconut Rice (see page 147).

LAYERED TOMATOES, ZUCCHINI, & POTATOES

Eggplant would work well here instead of the zucchini, as would a torn ball of mozzarella added alongside the Parmesan.

SERVES 4

3 zucchini, sliced into thick rounds

1½lb potatoes, peeled, and cut into ³/₈-inch slices

¹/₃ cup good-quality olive oil

2 garlic cloves, thinly sliced

28oz can plum tomatoes

1 teaspoon dried oregano

1oz basil, leaves picked and chopped

1oz parsley, leaves picked and chopped

1 cup grated Parmesan cheese

¾ cup fresh bread crumbs

1 tablespoon butter

salt and freshly ground black pepper

Place the sliced zucchini in a colander. Sprinkle with ½ teaspoon of salt, toss so all the slices are coated, and leave to drip over the sink for 30 minutes.

Preheat the oven to 350F°. Bring a large saucepan of salted water to a boil, and boil the potatoes until the outer edges are just tender (start checking after 2 minutes). Drain, and tip into a large roasting pan. Drizzle over 2 tablespoons of the olive oil, season, and roast in the oven for 25–35 minutes, until soft and turning golden.

Once the zucchini have finished draining, tip them into a second, deep roasting pan or ovenproof dish, toss with 2 tablespoons of the olive oil, and roast in the oven alongside the potatoes for 25–30 minutes until golden.

Meanwhile, heat the remaining tablespoon of oil in a large frying pan, add the garlic, and fry for a few minutes until just turning golden. Add the tomatoes and oregano, then season. Bring to a boil, and then turn down the heat, and simmer for 20 minutes. Stir through the basil and parsley and set aside.

Once the zucchini slices are cooked, top them with half the tomato sauce, followed by half the cheese, and all of the roasted potato slices. Spread the remaining tomato sauce over the top, sprinkle with the bread crumbs and remaining cheese, then dot with the butter. Bake for 20 minutes until golden and bubbling.

CORN CHOWDER

This soup is a lovely soft yellow; it sings with the color of spring, and gently soothes.

SERVES 4

FOR THE SOUP

1 tablespoon butter

1 tablespoon olive oil

small bunch of scallions, sliced

1 bay leaf

1 potato (approx. 10oz), peeled, and cut into small chunks

14fl oz milk

14fl oz vegetable stock

21oz canned whole kernel corn, drained

FOR THE CROÛTONS

2 slices of bread

1 tablespoon olive oil

2½oz cheddar cheese, coarsely grated

salt and freshly ground black pepper

Preheat the oven to 400°F. In a large saucepan, melt the butter with the olive oil over medium-low heat. When it starts to foam, add the scallions and bay leaf. Sweat for 4–5 minutes until they begin to soften.

Stir in the potato, then add the milk and stock. Bring just to a boil, then simmer for 10–12 minutes until the potato is tender. Add the corn, and cook for another 2 minutes to just warm it through. Discard the bay leaf. Blitz the soup until smooth using a blender. If it's too thick, thin it down with a little milk or water to your desired consistency.

Meanwhile, for the croûtons, tear the bread into smallish chunks, add to a baking sheet along with the olive oil, season, and bake in the oven for 10 minutes, until turning golden. Sprinkle over the cheese, and return to the oven for a few minutes until the cheese is oozy and bubbling.

Ladle the soup into bowls and top with the cheesy croûtons.

Tip: Try adding a little cayenne pepper or red pepper flakes to the soup for a warming kick.

WATER CHESTNUT & SHIITAKE DONBURI

This dish is inspired by the *yasai katsudon* I often ate with my neighbors when I was growing up. Our gardens were joined, so we were always nipping in and out. This dish reminds me of them.

SERVES 2

2 tablespoons butter

1 onion, sliced

4oz fresh shiitake mushrooms, thickly sliced

8oz can sliced water chestnuts, drained and roughly chopped

1 tablespoon grated (peeled) fresh ginger

1 tablespoon Marsala wine

3 tablespoons soy sauce

7fl oz fish stock

4 eggs, beaten

heaping ¾ cup jasmine rice, cooked according to package instructions

Tip: If you don't have jasmine rice, use basmati or other long grain instead.

Melt the butter in a small frying pan over medium heat, then add the onion, mushrooms, and water chestnuts. Fry, stirring often, until the onion is softening and the mushrooms and chestnuts are turning golden, about 5–10 minutes, then add the ginger, and cook for another 2 minutes.

Add the Marsala, soy sauce, and fish stock. Bring to a boil, then reduce the heat to a simmer. Tip in the eggs, swirl in a little, then cover and simmer for 1 minute. When you take the lid off, the eggs should remain a bit runny on top.

Divide the cooked rice between two bowls and top with the vegetable and egg mixture.

CORN, CHARD, & CHEESE TART

This is a great dish to prep ahead for a picnic, or to make at the start of the week to cut up and take into work for lunch.

SERVES 6

1 recipe Flaky Pie Crust Dough on page 150 (or 18–20oz ready-made flaky pie crust dough)

FOR THE FILLING

4 tablespoons butter

2 onions, thinly sliced

1 pinch of sumac

2 teaspoons red pepper flakes

8 sprigs of lemon thyme, leaves picked and chopped

7oz Swiss chard, thinly sliced

12oz canned whole kernel corn, drained, and half blitzed with a stick blender

7oz crème fraîche

3 eggs

3½oz feta cheese, crumbled

salt and freshly ground black pepper

salad, to serve

Tip: To blind bake; line the pie crust with parchment paper, then fill with uncooked rice, and bake in a preheated 400°F oven for 20 minutes. Remove the rice and paper and bake for another 10 minutes until lightly golden.

Preheat the oven to 350°F.

You'll need a loose-bottomed 10-inch tart pan. To make the filling: melt the butter in a large frying pan over medium heat, then add the onions with a pinch of salt, sumac, and half the red pepper flakes and lemon thyme. Turn the heat to low, then soften slowly for 30–35 minutes, until sticky and golden. Next, add the chard, and cook for another 4–5 minutes until it is wilted, and any excess moisture has evaporated. Season, and remove from the heat.

In a bowl, beat together the corn, crème fraîche and eggs, season, and then set aside. In a separate bowl, toss the feta with the remaining red pepper flakes and lemon thyme.

Roll the dough out so that it is about 2 inches larger than your tart pan. Carefully drape the dough into the pan, lightly pressing into the base and sides of the pan, then trim off the excess, and generously prick the base with a fork. Chill in the fridge for 20 minutes. Heat a baking sheet in the oven.

Blind bake (see tip), and then reduce the temperature to 325°F.

Tip the onion mixture into the pie crust, spread evenly across the base, then pour in the egg mixture. Scatter over the feta mixture, and bake in the oven for 25–30 minutes until just set in the middle and golden on top.

Allow to cool slightly before removing from the pan. Slice, and serve with a salad.

FISH

CRAB THORAN

I first had a Crab Thoran at a small Indian restaurant near where I grew up in South East London, and it still remains one of my favorite dishes. The combination of the sweet crab and coconut, with the earthy mustard seeds, and the warmth from the ginger and chile is really delicious.

SERVES 2 AS A STARTER OR SMALL LUNCH

2 tablespoons flavorless oil (such as sunflower)

½ tablespoon brown or black mustard seeds

1 teaspoon fenugreek seeds

2 shallots, minced

½ tablespoon grated (peeled) fresh ginger

1 green chile, finely chopped

20 fresh or dried curry leaves

2 tomatoes, chopped and seeded

⅓ cup dried, shredded coconut, steeped in boiling water for 10 minutes

2 × 6oz cans lump crabmeat, drained

1 lime, cut into wedges, to serve

Heat the oil in a frying pan over high heat, then add the mustard seeds. Wait until they start to pop (about 30 seconds), and then add the fenugreek seeds. Fry very briefly until fragrant. Reduce the heat to low, and add the shallots, ginger, and chile. Fry, stirring often, for another 5–10 minutes, or until the shallots are softening and golden.

Add the curry leaves, tomatoes, and coconut (along with the soaking liquid). Cook for a few minutes until the tomatoes are starting to break down, then carefully stir through the crabmeat and serve, garnished with a lime wedge.

This dish goes well with the Quick Chapatis on page 146 or Coconut Rice on page 147.

HERBY TUNA & NAVY BEAN SALAD

This salad is super simple; it's delicious served immediately, but also works really well the next day for lunch.

SERVES 2

FOR THE DRESSING

1 teaspoon Dijon mustard

2 teaspoons vinegar (white wine or cider)

1 tablespoon olive oil

zest of 1 lemon

1 shallot, minced

½oz dill, leaves picked and finely chopped

5oz can tuna in olive oil, drained

14oz can navy beans, drained and rinsed

1 small cucumber, peeled, seeded, and thinly sliced

salt and freshly ground black pepper

bread or toast, to serve

Start by making the dressing: whisk the mustard, vinegar, and oil together. Season, and then stir in the lemon zest, shallot, and dill.

In a separate bowl, mix the tuna, beans, and cucumber together, then pour over the dressing and toss lightly to combine. This is best served with a slice of bread or toast to mop up all the juices.

SALMON FISH CAKES WITH SAUERKRAUT

When I was a child, I used to go for lunch at Ruth's, a family friend. I have fond memories of her little salmon fish cakes; to my 5-year-old's mind, there were mountains of them. I felt such anticipation as the plate was passed through the kitchen hatch.

SERVES 4

2 × 6oz cans skinless and boneless red or pink salmon, drained

14oz floury potatoes (russet are great), boiled, cooled, and roughly mashed

2 shallots (or ½ onion), minced

1 teaspoon caraway seeds

zest of 1 lemon (then lemon sliced into wedges to serve)

all-purpose flour, for dusting

2 teaspoons flavorless oil (such as sunflower), plus more if needed

3 tablespoons salted butter

4 heaping tablespoons jarred sauerkraut

4 tablespoons sour cream

salt and freshly ground black pepper

Tips:
Try sprinkling the finished dish with some chopped dill or parsley.

You can flavor these in a multitude of ways: try adding some thinly sliced lime leaf and finely chopped chile, and serve with lime wedges. For an Indian twist, mix in some ground turmeric and cumin, and thinly sliced curry leaf, then serve with a dollop of yogurt or mango chutney.

Mix together the salmon, potatoes, shallots (or onion), ½ teaspoon of the caraway seeds and the lemon zest, then season. Shape into eight small patties. Chill the fish cakes in the fridge for 20 minutes to firm up.

Just before cooking, dust the tops and bottoms of the fish cakes in a little flour. Heat the oil in a frying pan over medium heat, then add the fish cakes. Cook for 6–7 minutes per side until golden, then roll the sides across the pan briefly to brown, too.

Melt the butter in a separate small frying pan. When it starts to foam, add the remaining caraway seeds. Fry briefly until the butter smells nutty and is beginning to brown.

To serve, divide the fish cakes between four plates and top with the sauerkraut and soured cream. Drizzle over a little of the fragrant butter, and liberally squeeze with the lemon wedges at the table.

ANCHOVY PASTA WITH STICKY ONIONS

Canned anchovies are magic; they can be melted into a multitude of things to create an extra depth of salty complexity, which they do here in this comforting pasta dish.

SERVES 4

1 tablespoon olive oil

2 heaping tablespoons butter

3 onions, finely sliced

2 garlic cloves, minced

2oz can anchovy fillets, drained and finely chopped

²/₃ cup milk

14oz spaghetti

a handful of parsley, chopped

salt and freshly ground black pepper

Tip: Try with the Bread Crumb Topping on page 155.

Add the olive oil and butter to a large frying pan over medium heat. Tip in the onions and garlic, turn the heat to low, and sweat slowly for 20–25 minutes until soft and golden, stirring often.

Once the onions have turned golden, add the anchovies. Allow them to melt away into the onion mixture, then stir in the milk, season, and continue to cook for about 5–10 minutes. Once the onion mixture has started to break down, remove from the heat, and roughly mash.

Meanwhile, boil the pasta in a pan of salted water according to the package instructions, or until tender, reserve a mug of the cooking water, then drain.

Tip the pasta straight into the sauce along with most of the parsley and enough of the reserved cooking water to make the sauce coat the pasta, tossing to mix. Divide between four plates, and sprinkle with the remaining parsley.

SMOKED MACKEREL PÂTÉ & QUICK PICKLES

This quick and simple pâté is perfect as an appetizer, or can be boxed up and taken for lunch. Try adding a little minced shallot or onion to the quick pickles for added punch.

SERVES 2

FOR THE QUICK PICKLES

½ large cucumber, sliced into rounds

1 teaspoon salt

2 tablespoons white wine vinegar

½ teaspoon coriander seeds, lightly crushed

½ teaspoon fennel seeds, lightly crushed

2 tablespoons superfine sugar

FOR THE PÂTÉ

8oz canned smoked mackerel fillets in oil, drained

3½oz crème fraîche

juice of ½ lemon

½ teaspoon fennel seeds, lightly crushed

sea salt and freshly ground black pepper

toast, to serve

Start by making the quick pickles: place the cucumber in a strainer, and sprinkle with the salt. Leave to stand over the sink (or a bowl) for 20 minutes. Squeeze to get rid of any excess moisture, and pat dry.

Meanwhile, in a bowl, mix together the vinegar, coriander and fennel seeds, and all the sugar, stirring until the sugar has dissolved. Submerge the cucumber slices. They can be eaten immediately, or will keep, covered, in the fridge for a few days.

To make the pâté, mash the mackerel fillets with the crème fraîche, lemon juice, and fennel seeds. Season, and enjoy spread on toast, topped with the quick pickles.

A SRI LANKAN MACKEREL CURRY

I went to Sri Lanka nearly ten years ago, but the flavors of the food have stayed with me. I often revisit my notebook with the recipes I scribbled down while watching people cook there. This recipe draws on those flavors.

SERVES 4

13oz canned mackerel in sunflower oil, drained, and 2 tablespoons oil reserved

1 teaspoon brown or black mustard seeds

1 teaspoon fenugreek seeds

3 cardamom pods, bashed

1 onion, finely sliced

1 tablespoon grated (peeled) fresh ginger

5 garlic cloves, minced

1 red chile, finely chopped and seeds left in for more heat, if liked

15–20 fresh or dried curry leaves

28oz can plum tomatoes

scant ½ cup coconut milk

salt and freshly ground black pepper

rice or chapatis, to serve

Heat the reserved mackerel oil in a saucepan over high heat, then add the mustard seeds. When they start to pop (about 30 seconds), add the fenugreek seeds and cardamom pods. Fry briefly until fragrant, then reduce the heat to medium-low and add the onion with a pinch of salt. Sweat the mixture gently for 10–15 minutes, until soft and tinged golden.

Add the ginger, garlic, chile, and curry leaves, then fry for 1–2 minutes. Add the tomatoes, and season. Bring to a boil, then simmer over medium heat for 15 minutes until thickened slightly.

Gently add the mackerel, taking care to keep the pieces whole, reduce the heat to low, and cook for 10 minutes to warm the mackerel through. Just before serving, stir in the coconut milk. Serve alongside rice or Quick Chapatis (see page 146).

CRAB FRIED RICE

Fresh crab is something a bit special and often expensive, not to mention awkward. Canned crab is delicious, and a fraction of the price of fresh. I often make fried rice: it's a great vehicle for pretty much anything! If you live near a Chinese supermarket, explore all the different chili oils available. Lao Gan Ma Black Bean Chili Oil is a personal favorite.

SERVES 4

1 tablespoon flavorless oil, such as sunflower

7oz green beans, cut into 1¼-inch pieces

4 garlic cloves, minced

7oz jasmine rice, cooked and cooled (or use any leftover rice)

1 teaspoon chili oil, plus extra to serve

2 tablespoons soy sauce

small bunch of scallions, sliced, whites and greens separated

2 eggs, beaten

2 × 6oz cans lump crabmeat, drained

2 teaspoons toasted sesame oil

In a large frying pan or wok, heat the sunflower oil over medium heat. Once hot, add the green beans. Fry for 3–4 minutes until starting to color, then add the garlic, rice, chili oil, soy sauce, and scallion whites. Fry, stirring often, until the rice has heated through, about 3–4 minutes.

Push the rice mixture to one side of the pan, and pour the beaten eggs into the space. Allow the eggs to begin to set, then pull the sides into the middle, ensuring all the egg comes into contact with the pan. Once it is all cooked, use a spatula to break it into pieces, and stir into the rice mixture. Turn off the heat, and stir through the crabmeat and sesame oil.

Pile into bowls and top with the sliced scallion greens and an extra drop of chili oil, if you fancy.

Tip: Feel free to leave the eggs out completely or try frying four eggs in a little oil to top the rice instead.

POTATO LATKES WITH SALMON PÂTÉ

Latkes are a thing of my childhood; one of two things (the other being doughnuts) that made Hanukkah vaguely interesting to me as a small child. Here they are served alongside a twist on the classic sour cream. I like to have a few pickles to nibble on, too.

SERVES 2 (MAKES ABOUT 8)

FOR THE LATKES

1 onion, coarsely grated

18oz Yukon Gold potatoes, peeled and coarsely grated

1 egg

½ tablespoon all-purpose flour

3 tablespoons flavorless oil (such as sunflower)

FOR THE PÂTÉ

6oz can skinless and boneless red or pink salmon, drained

4 tablespoons sour cream

1 teaspoon finely chopped tarragon

zest of 1 lemon, plus 1 teaspoon juice

salt and freshly ground black pepper

gherkins, to serve

Put the grated onion and potatoes in a clean dish towel, then squeeze out as much liquid as you can. Tip the potato and onion into a large bowl, add the egg and flour, season, and then mix everything together. Set aside.

To make the salmon pâté: in a small bowl, mix together the salmon, sour cream, tarragon, and lemon zest and juice, then season and set aside.

When you're ready to cook your latkes, heat the oil in a large frying pan over medium heat. Once hot, drop in heaping tablespoons of the potato mixture, and flatten each slightly with a spatula. Fry for a few minutes per side, until golden and crisp (you may need to cook them in batches). Drain on paper towels and then transfer to a plate or rack while you finish cooking the remaining latkes.

To serve, divide the latkes between plates and top with the salmon pâté and a few gherkins, if you like.

CRAB LINGUINE WITH CHERRY TOMATOES

Cherry tomatoes and crab are a great combination. Using peeled cherry tomatoes is preferable, as the skins can be a bit tough. The sweetness is married with the heady aniseed flavor of fennel, the tang from the lemon, and a tingle of warmth from the red pepper flakes.

SERVES 2

1 tablespoon olive oil

2 garlic cloves, sliced

pinch of red pepper flakes

pinch of fennel seeds

14oz can peeled cherry tomatoes, drained

7oz linguine

6oz can lump crabmeat, drained

zest and juice of ½ lemon

a handful of basil, leaves picked and thinly sliced

salt and freshly ground black pepper

Heat the oil in a large frying pan over medium heat, then add the garlic, red pepper flakes, and fennel seeds. Fry for a few minutes, until the garlic is smelling fragrant and tinged golden. Add the tomatoes, season, and continue to cook for 10 minutes until thickened a little, but with the tomatoes still holding some shape.

Meanwhile, boil the linguine in a pan of salted water according to the package instructions, or until tender, reserve a mug of the cooking water, then drain.

Add the linguine and crab to the sauce, gently fold together, and finish by adding the lemon zest and juice, with enough of the reserved cooking water to make the sauce coat the pasta.

Pile the pasta onto two plates, and serve with a scattering of basil, if you like.

SMOKED MACKEREL KEDGEREE

My granny always made a very decadent kedgeree for brunch gatherings when I was growing up. The sweet and mildly spiced rice is sumptuous with the smoky fish.

SERVES 4

10½oz basmati rice, rinsed

1 heaping tablespoon butter

8oz canned smoked mackerel in oil, drained, and 2 tablespoons oil reserved, broken into large chunks

2 onions, chopped

1 green chile, finely chopped and seeded

4 cardamom pods, bashed

2 bay leaves

1 tablespoon mild curry powder

3 eggs, boiled to your preference, peeled and quartered

salt

1 lemon, cut into wedges, to serve

Tip: Try scattering with fresh cilantro and a spoonful of yogurt.

Boil the rice in plenty of boiling, salted water, according to package instructions, drain, and rinse under cold running water, then set aside.

In a large frying pan, melt the butter with the reserved mackerel oil over medium-low heat. Add the onions, chile, cardamom pods, and bay leaves, turn the heat to low, and soften gently for 15 minutes.

Add the curry powder, and cook for another 30 seconds. Stir in the rice to warm through, then add the fish chunks, and gently toss together, taking care not to break up the fish too much. Top with the eggs and serve with the lemon wedges.

Watch out for the cardamom pods and bay leaves when eating.

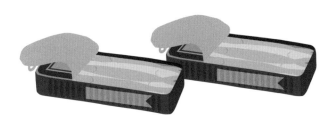

SICILIAN SARDINES ON TOAST

Taking inspiration from the flavors of Sicily and the very British dish of Welsh rarebit, this speedy supper was born.

SERVES 2

2 × 3¾oz cans sardines in oil, drained

1 egg yolk

zest of 1 lemon (and then cut lemon into wedges)

pinch of red pepper flakes

pinch of fennel seeds

¼ cup pine nuts, toasted and chopped

¼ cup golden raisins, chopped

scant ²/₃ cup ricotta cheese

4 slices of bread

salt and freshly ground black pepper

Tip: Try adding fennel: very finely slice a fennel bulb, toss with a little olive oil and lemon juice, season, and place on top of the toast when it comes out from under the broiler.

Preheat your broiler to high.

In a large bowl, using a fork, mash the sardines with the egg yolk, lemon zest, red pepper flakes, fennel seeds, pine nuts, golden raisins and ricotta, then season. Lightly toast your bread, and then spread with the sardine mixture. Place on a baking sheet, and broil until a golden crust forms. Serve with the lemon wedges.

SARDINE & LEMON LINGUINE

I am a total sardine convert. In this recipe, the rich and oily sardines are balanced with sweet onion, sharp lemon and the crunch of warm, garlicky bread crumbs. I challenge you to make this even if you think you hate fishy fish!

SERVES 2

1 tablespoon olive oil

3¾oz can sardines in olive oil, drained, and oil reserved

1 onion, finely sliced

2 garlic cloves, finely sliced

pinch of red pepper flakes

sprig of rosemary

7oz linguine (or spaghetti)

zest and juice of 1 lemon

½ quantity Bread Crumb Topping (page 155)

salt

Heat the olive oil and the reserved oil from the sardines in a heavy-based frying pan over medium heat, then add the onion, garlic, red pepper flakes, and rosemary. Turn the heat to low, and fry slowly until sweet, sticky, and golden (this should take about 15–20 minutes).

When the onion is nearly done, boil the pasta in a pan of salted water according to the package instructions, or until tender, reserve a mug of the cooking water, then drain.

Tip the pasta into the sauce, then mash in the sardines, and add the lemon zest and juice, along with enough of the reserved cooking water to make the sauce coat the pasta.

Mound the pasta onto plates and liberally sprinkle with the golden bread crumbs.

VIETNAMESE CRAB CAKES

These are inspired by a Vietnamese dish of fish marinated in lots of turmeric, ginger, and garlic, pan-fried and served with the classic Vietnamese dressing *Nước chấm*. I've translated these flavors into crisp crab cakes.

SERVES 2

FOR THE CRAB CAKES

2 × 6oz cans lump crabmeat, drained

1-inch piece of fresh ginger, peeled and grated (about 1½ tablespoons when grated)

1 red chile, seeded and finely chopped

1 garlic clove, minced

½ cup fresh dill, finely chopped

1 teaspoon ground turmeric

2 shallots, minced

²/₃ cup dried bread crumbs

2 eggs, beaten

1 tablespoon flavorless oil (such as sunflower)

FOR THE DRESSING

4 teaspoons fish sauce

juice of 1 lime

4 teaspoons soft brown sugar

1 red chile, seeded and finely chopped

1 garlic clove, minced

To make the crab cakes, mix the crab, ginger, chile, garlic, dill, turmeric, shallots, 4 tablespoons of the bread crumbs and half the beaten eggs in a bowl. Shape into eight patties, and stick in the fridge to firm up for at least 20 minutes.

To make the dressing, mix all the ingredients with 2 tablespoons of water, check the balance of sour, sweet, and salty, and adjust accordingly.

Just before frying, dip each cake in the remaining beaten egg, and then into the remaining bread crumbs to coat. Heat the oil in a large frying pan over medium heat, and fry the cakes for 4 minutes per side until golden.

Serve alongside the dressing, for drizzling or dunking.

Tip: Try nestling a crab cake in a lettuce leaf with some finely sliced cucumber, then drizzle with the dressing.

ANCHOVY MAC 'N' CHEESE

Mac 'n' cheese is a classic and a favorite of mine. It's taken to another level here with the addition of salty anchovies, sweet onion, and bay leaves.

SERVES 4

4 tablespoons butter

7 canned anchovy fillets, drained and finely chopped

1 onion, minced

3 bay leaves

12oz macaroni

6 tablespoons all-purpose flour

2¾ cups whole milk

12oz aged Cheddar cheese, grated

3oz fresh bread crumbs (from about 2 slices)

1 large tomato, sliced

salt

Worcestershire sauce, to serve

Tip: Try substituting some of the macaroni pasta for blanched cauliflower florets for something a little lighter.

Preheat the oven to 400°F.

To make the sauce, melt the butter with the anchovies in a frying pan over low heat, then add the onion and bay leaves, and cook gently for about 20–25 minutes, until the onion is very soft.

Meanwhile, boil the pasta in a pan of salted water according to package instructions, or until tender, then drain and rinse under cold water. Set aside.

Once the onion is soft, stir in the flour, and continue to cook for 2 minutes. Next, add the milk, a little at a time, stirring to incorporate before adding more. Cook, stirring often, until the sauce has thickened a little. Remove from the heat, and melt in two-thirds of the cheese. Carefully remove the bay leaves. Mix the remaining cheese with the bread crumbs.

Tip the pasta into an ovenproof dish (roughly 12 x 8 inches), then pour the sauce over and mix to combine. Top with the bread crumb/cheese mixture and sliced tomato. Bake for 25–35 minutes until golden, and bubbling vigorously.

Serve with a generous amount of Worcestershire sauce.

TUNA, TOMATOES, & GNOCCHI

This dish is very quick to make, satisfying, and delicious. If you can't find or don't fancy gnocchi, it can be substituted for cooked dried pasta such as penne.

SERVES 4

2 tablespoons olive oil

1 red onion, minced

½ teaspoon red pepper flakes

pinch of ground cinnamon

28oz can of chopped tomatoes

2 tablespoons capers, drained

2 × 5oz cans of tuna in oil, drained

18oz fresh gnocchi

zest and juice of ½ lemon

8-9oz fresh mozzarella cheese ball, drained and roughly torn

salt and freshly ground black pepper

Tips:
This recipe is extra yummy with a pinch of fennel seeds added along with the red pepper flakes. If you don't have capers, pitted olives would also work really well. You could also throw in some chopped basil or parsley.

If you don't have mozzarella, top with grated Parmesan or Cheddar cheese instead.

Preheat the oven to 400°F.

Heat the oil in a frying pan over medium heat, then add the onion, red pepper flakes, and cinnamon. Turn the heat to low, and sweat for 10–15 minutes, or until soft and beginning to turn golden. Add the tomatoes, capers, and tuna, and season. Bring to a boil, and then simmer over medium heat for 20 minutes.

Meanwhile, boil your gnocchi in a pan of salted water for 1 minute, then drain.

Tip the gnocchi into the sauce, then add the lemon zest and juice. Transfer everything into a baking dish, and top with the mozzarella, then bake for 20 minutes until golden and bubbling.

ROASTED POTATO & TUNA NIÇOISE

A classic salad niçoise centers around tomatoes, anchovies, olives, and olive oil, with other additions being at the whim of the maker. So, this is my perfect niçoise.

SERVES 4

1½lb small new potatoes, large ones halved

6 tablespoons olive oil

7oz fine green beans, halved

2 tablespoons capers, drained

6 canned anchovy fillets, drained and finely chopped

1 tablespoon Dijon mustard

1 garlic clove, minced

2 tablespoons white wine vinegar

2 Little Gem butterhead lettuce, leaves separated, and large ones sliced

2 × 5oz cans tuna in olive oil, drained and flaked

a handful of basil leaves, thinly sliced

3 tablespoons finely chopped chives

salt and freshly ground black pepper

Preheat the oven to 350°F.

Toss the potatoes in a roasting pan with 2 tablespoons of the oil and a splash of water, season and roast for 30–40 minutes, or until golden and tender.

Meanwhile, boil the beans for about 5 minutes, until just tender, then drain and refresh under cold water. To make the dressing, mix together the capers, anchovy fillets, mustard, garlic, vinegar, and the remaining olive oil, then season.

Mix the warm potatoes with the dressing, and then tip into a serving dish. Toss with the lettuce, green beans, and tuna, then sprinkle over the herbs.

Serve immediately to prevent the lettuce wilting. This dish does work really well as a packed lunch, too: keep the lettuce separate until you're about to eat.

TUNA & FLAGEOLET BEAN PASTA

The sweetness of the slowly cooked garlic, in partnership with the warmth of the chile, combines perfectly with the delicate flageolet beans and tuna.

SERVES 4

2 tablespoons olive oil

2 garlic cloves, finely sliced

1 red chile, seeded and finely chopped

14oz spaghetti or linguine

14oz can flageolet beans, drained and rinsed

2 × 5oz cans tuna in olive oil, drained

bunch of parsley, chopped

zest and juice of ½ lemon, plus extra to serve

salt and freshly ground black pepper

Heat the olive oil in a large frying pan over low heat, then stir in the garlic and chile, and fry very gently until the garlic is soft and lightly golden, about 5–10 minutes.

Meanwhile, boil the pasta in a pan of salted water according to package instructions, or until tender. Reserve a mug of the cooking water, then drain.

Add the beans to the frying pan, increase the heat to medium, and warm through for 4–5 minutes. Add the drained pasta, tuna, parsley, and lemon zest and juice, with enough of the reserved cooking water to coat the pasta in the sauce. Season generously with black pepper, and toss to combine. Serve piled high with an extra squeeze of lemon.

SPRATS WITH SWEET & SOUR BEETS

Cooking beets in this way is so quick; the sweetness of the butter offsets its earthiness perfectly. You could try topping the fish-laden toast with a poached egg to make this into a more substantial dinner. Sprats are also called Brisling sardines.

SERVES 2 AS A LIGHT DINNER OR LUNCH

2 tablespoons butter

1 teaspoon caraway seeds

2 large raw beets, peeled, and coarsely grated

2 large gherkins, sliced, plus 2 tablespoons of the pickling liquid

2 thick slices of bread

3½oz can sprats (brisling sardines) in oil, drained and flaked

2 tablespoons sour cream

salt and freshly ground black pepper

Melt the butter in a frying pan over medium-high heat. When it's foaming, add the caraway seeds, and cook for 30 seconds.

Next, add the grated beets, and fry for 3 minutes. Add the gherkin pickling liquid, and cook for 1 additional minute, then season, and turn off the heat.

Toast the bread, then top with the beets, flaked sprats, and sliced gherkins. Serve sour cream alongside.

MACKEREL TACOS

My citrus-laden salsa and the spicy sour cream are best friends with the smoky mackerel. These are fun, quick, and easy to rustle up, perfect for sharing with friends and a cold beer.

SERVES 4

½ small red cabbage, thinly sliced

1 teaspoon fine salt

2 ripe avocados, peeled, pitted and sliced

8 small corn tortillas

12oz canned smoked mackerel fillets in oil, drained and flaked into large chunks

freshly ground black pepper

FOR THE SALSA

4 tomatoes, seeded and roughly chopped

1 small red onion, minced

large bunch of cilantro, roughly chopped

juice of 2 limes

FOR THE SPICY SOUR CREAM

½ cup sour cream

2 tablespoons hot sauce (or more if you like heat)

Put the cabbage into a colander, and sprinkle over the salt. Rub it all over the cabbage, and leave to drain over the sink for 20 minutes.

To make the salsa, put the tomatoes in a bowl and mix in the onion, cilantro, and half the lime juice, then season with black pepper, and set aside. In another bowl, mix the sour cream with the hot sauce for your spicy sour cream. Toss the avocado with the remaining lime juice.

Squeeze any excess moisture out of the cabbage, then tip into a clean bowl.

Heat a large griddle or frying pan, then cook the tortillas for 30 seconds or so per side, until warm and with brown spots. Stick the stack of warm tortillas on the table with the bowls of spicy sour cream, salsa, cabbage, avocado, and the flaked mackerel, layer up and enjoy.

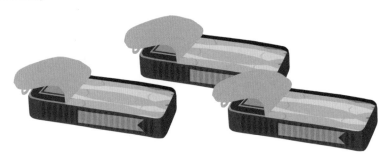

APPLE, FENNEL, & CRAB SALAD

This salad is light, crisp, sweet, and sharp, with a spicy kick from the chile and ginger. It makes a lovely light supper for summer evenings.

SERVES 2

FOR THE DRESSING

1 teaspoon grated (peeled) fresh ginger

1 shallot, minced

1 tablespoon cider vinegar

1 tablespoon olive oil

1 red chile, seeded and finely chopped

salt and freshly ground black pepper

1 fennel bulb, very thinly sliced

1 pink grapefruit, peeled and sectioned

1 Granny Smith apple, quartered, cored, and thinly sliced

6oz can lump crabmeat, drained

To make the dressing, mix together the ginger, shallot, vinegar, olive oil, and chile, then season.

Tip the fennel, grapefruit, and apple into a large bowl, add the dressing, and toss to coat.

Divide between two plates and top each with some crab.

FRUIT & SWEET CANS

PEAR & YOGURT PANCAKES

Delicious fluffy pancakes are a great breakfast. I like adding frozen raspberries or blackberries to the pears, and drizzling everything with a crazy amount of maple syrup.

SERVES 4 (MAKES ABOUT 12 PANCAKES)

11oz plain yogurt, plus extra to serve

2 eggs

1½ cups all-purpose flour

1 teaspoon baking soda

pinch of ground cinnamon

1 teaspoon sugar

14oz can pears in juice, sliced into wedges and juice reserved

juice of 1 lemon

pinch of ground nutmeg

1 tablespoon butter, plus extra for frying

salt

To make the pancakes, combine the yogurt and eggs in a jug. In a large bowl, mix the flour, baking soda, cinnamon, a pinch of salt, and half the sugar, then whisk in the contents of the jug to make a smooth batter.

In a small saucepan, add the pears and the reserved juice with the lemon juice, remaining sugar, and the nutmeg. Bring to a boil and cook for about 5 minutes until the pears are soft, and the liquid has largely evaporated. Stir in the butter, then set aside.

Melt a little butter in a large frying pan over medium heat, then dollop in a heaped tablespoon of the batter for each pancake, and cook for 2–3 minutes per side until golden and springy. You will most likely need to do this in batches.

To serve, divide the pancakes between four plates, and top with the pear compote and a little extra yogurt, if you like.

MANGO & CARDAMOM LASSI

Cool, sweet and fruity; this lassi is a perfect partner to a curry or anything else spicy. You can also have it for breakfast topped with granola and fruit.

SERVES 2

7oz plain yogurt

7oz canned mango purée (or equivalent of canned mango slices)

a small handful of ice cubes (about 6 or so)

2 cardamom pods, seeds removed and crushed

Put all your ingredients in a blender and whizz until smooth. Pour into glasses and enjoy immediately.

Tip: This lassi is thick, so if you want a thinner drink, simply stir in a little cold water or milk.

PEACH & RASPBERRY LAYERED PUDDING

This falls somewhere between a trifle and a tiramisu, and both in my view are delicious. Try playing with the fruit, alcohol, and cake to shape this to your preferences.

SERVES 6

15oz can raspberries in syrup

zest and juice of ½ lemon

1 drop rose water (optional)

3½ tablespoons superfine sugar

15oz can peach slices, drained

small plain sponge cake (about 9oz)

6 tablespoons sweet alcohol (cassis, Chambord, fruit brandy, or Marsala all work well)

9oz mascarpone cheese

1 extra-large egg, separated

generous 1 cup heavy cream

salt

In a saucepan, mix together the raspberries (and their syrup), lemon juice, rose water, if using, 1½ tablespoons of the sugar, and a small pinch of salt. Place over medium heat for about 5 minutes to thicken a little, then stir in the peach slices. Leave to cool while you prepare the rest of the pudding.

Cut the sponge cake into flat ³/₈-inch slices (as if you're cutting a loaf of bread), and lay in a large bowl or dish. Douse in the sweet alcohol, and allow it to soak in thoroughly. In a bowl, beat the mascarpone with the remaining sugar and the egg yolk until smooth. In another bowl, whisk the egg white to stiff peaks, then fold that into the mascarpone. Finally, in a third bowl, whip the cream to soft peaks and then fold it into the mascarpone mixture.

Top the soaked sponge cake with the fruit from the pan, and then carefully spoon over the mascarpone mixture (you want to try to avoid knocking all of the air out of it), and spread into an evenish layer. Cover and refrigerate for 1 hour or so before eating. Serve, topped with the lemon zest.

PRUNE & GINGER MUFFINS

This recipe is for my dad who loves ginger cake. These muffins are gloriously sticky, and perfect for a weekend breakfast, either served warm, spread with butter, or cold with a cup of tea.

MAKES 12

^{1}/$_3$ cup golden syrup

4 heaping tablespoons molasses

scant ½ cup slightly salted butter

^{1}/$_3$ cup dark brown sugar

1^1/$_3$ cups self-rising flour

½ teaspoon baking powder

2 teaspoons ground ginger

1 teaspoon ground cinnamon

2 eggs, beaten

scant ¼ cup milk

¾ cup walnuts, roughly chopped

10½oz can prunes, drained and chopped

Preheat the oven to 325°F and line a 12-hole muffin pan with paper cupcake cups.

Put the golden syrup, molasses, and butter in a saucepan over low heat, and melt them together. Add the sugar, and continue to heat for 1 minute, then set aside to cool a little.

Mix the flour, baking powder, and spices in a large bowl. Pour in the contents of the saucepan, followed by the eggs, milk, walnuts, and prunes, and stir briefly to mix.

Divide the mixture between the muffin cups, and bake for 25–30 minutes until well-risen, and they spring back up when pressed gently. Allow to cool briefly in the pan before eating, or popping onto a wire rack to cool completely; they'll keep in an airtight container for up to 5 days.

FIG & ORANGE BLOSSOM FOOL

This very simple dessert is inspired by the sticky baklava I get from the Turkish shop at the end of my road: rich, floral, and thoroughly addictive.

SERVES 4

²/₃ cup light cream

scant ½ cup Greek yogurt

1 drop orange blossom water (or the zest of ½ orange, or both)

14oz canned figs in syrup, drained, and 2 tablespoons syrup reserved, figs roughly chopped

2 tablespoons toasted unsalted pistachios, roughly chopped

zest of ½ orange (optional)

In a bowl, whip the cream to soft peaks, then gently fold in the yogurt, orange blossom water, figs, and reserved syrup.

Divide the mixture between four tumblers or ramekins, and top with the pistachios just before serving. Sprinkle over a little extra orange zest, if you like.

Tip: If you can't get hold of figs, use canned prunes in syrup instead.

NO-CHURN RICE PUDDING ICE CREAM

Rice pudding is one of my all-time favorites. Give me any excuse to make or eat it, and I will. Here it's transformed into an Indian-inspired ice cream, bringing back memories of my trip to Rajasthan, where drinking ginger-heavy tea was the start to every day.

SERVES 8

2²/₃ cups (21fl oz) heavy cream

1 cinnamon stick

7 black peppercorns

3 cardamom pods

½ teaspoon fennel seeds

1oz fresh ginger (about 1-inch piece), peeled and sliced

14oz can ready-to-eat rice pudding

½ cup condensed milk

1 tablespoon rum or brandy

Tip: Try adding chopped almonds or pistachios to your mixture, or a tea bag at the infusing stage to make chai tea ice cream.

Put the cream into a heavy-based saucepan with all the spices. Bring to just below a boil, stirring regularly, then turn off the heat, cover, and leave to cool and infuse.

Once cooled, refrigerate until completely cold (if it isn't, it won't whip, so make sure it is fridge-cold). Strain into a bowl, and whip into soft peaks, then gently fold in the rice pudding, condensed milk, and rum or brandy. Transfer to a covered container, and freeze for at least 4–6 hours. Take out of the freezer, and pop into the fridge to soften slowly for 40 minutes before serving.

PEAR & PRUNE COBBLER

Sweet and sticky, with a hit of fiery ginger, this is just the ticket for chillier days, doused in a healthy amount of cream.

SERVES 6–8

3 × 14oz cans pears in juice, drained and cut into quarters

10½oz can prunes in juice (not drained)

6 pieces stem ginger in syrup, finely chopped

juice of 1 lemon

½ cup soft brown sugar

4½oz (1⅛ sticks) slightly salted cold butter, cut into small cubes

1⅞ cups self-rising flour

½ cup almonds (or pecans or hazelnuts), roughly chopped

cream or ice cream, to serve

Preheat the oven to 350°F.

In a baking dish (roughly 1½ quarts in capacity) mix the pears, prunes (and their juice), stem ginger, lemon juice, and ¼ cup of the sugar. Bake in the oven for 10 minutes.

Meanwhile, to make the topping, in a large bowl, rub the butter into the flour until it resembles fine bread crumbs. Stir in the remaining sugar and the nuts. Add 2–3 tablespoons cold water, and using your hands bring together into a dough.

Remove the fruit from the oven. Using your hands, roll the dough into small balls, then sit them on top of the fruit, leaving space in between each ball. Return to the oven for 25–30 minutes, until the topping is golden and puffed up, and the fruit below is bubbling. Serve immediately with scoops of ice cream, or a river of cream.

BANOFFEE PIE WITH HAZELNUT CREAM

What's not to love about sweet banana, a buttery cookie crust, and a load of nutty, chocolate cream? I feel my Granny Susan, who ate bananas with heavy cream and a sprinkling of superfine sugar, would agree.

SERVES 8

FOR THE CRUST

12oz (48 squares) graham crackers

7oz (1¾ sticks) slightly salted butter, melted

¾ cup blanched hazelnuts, toasted and finely chopped

FOR THE CARAMEL FILLING

generous ½ cup superfine sugar

14oz can condensed milk

4½ oz (1¹/₈ sticks) slightly salted butter, cut into small pieces

FOR THE TOP

3–4 bananas

squeeze of lemon juice

1¼ cups heavy cream

3 tablespoons Nutella

Begin with the crust: in a food-processor, blitz the graham crackers until you have fine crumbs (alternatively, put into a freezer bag, and whack with a rolling pin). Tip into a bowl with the melted butter and three quarters of the chopped hazelnuts, and mix to combine. Press the mixture into a 10-inch loose-bottomed tart pan, then pop in the fridge while you make the filling.

For the filling: add the sugar to a large, nonstick frying pan, put over medium-low heat, and allow to melt: do not stir! Once melted, turn up the heat, and simmer hard until it has turned a deep, golden color. Turn the heat to low, and slowly stir in the condensed milk. It may not come together immediately; keep stirring, and it will become smooth and uniform in color, about 10 minutes. Add the butter, stirring until melted and combined. Pour into your chilled crust, smooth the surface and put back into the fridge for at least 1 hour.

When you're ready to serve, peel and slice the bananas, toss with a little lemon juice (this will stop them going brown), and place over the caramel. Whip the cream to soft peaks, fold in the Nutella, then spread over the bananas. Sprinkle over the reserved hazelnuts to serve.

Tip: If you've got time to spare and prefer a less labor intensive approach, an alternative method for the caramel layer is to place the unopened can of condensed milk in a saucepan. Cover with boiling water, then simmer over low heat, uncovered (checking the water level remains at least 1 inch above the can) for about 3 hours. Allow to cool completely before opening, and tipping the contents into the prepared crust.

ROCKY ROAD WITH FIGS & WALNUTS

Rocky road's traditional marshmallow stickiness has been replaced by canned figs in this recipe. Sweet and juicy, they work perfectly with the rich, dark chocolate and almondy crunch of amaretti cookies.

MAKES 10 BARS

6oz (1½ sticks) slightly salted butter, diced

12oz dark chocolate, broken into squares

4 tablespoons golden syrup

4oz (1 cup) walnuts, toasted and roughly chopped

4oz amaretti cookies, broken into small pieces (vanilla wafers, Lotus Biscoff, or butter cookies would also work well)

14oz can figs in syrup, drained and chopped

Line an 8-inch square brownie pan with parchment paper.

In a medium saucepan, slowly melt together the butter, chocolate, and golden syrup, then fold in most of the walnuts, cookies and figs. Tip into the prepared pan, spreading evenly, and top with the reserved ingredients. Chill in the fridge to firm up (about 2–3 hours minimum) before cutting into bars.

COCONUT MILK PANNA COTTA

I love panna cotta, it's such a simple and delicious pudding. This coconut panna cotta is a tropical variety, served up with juicy, sweet pineapple. Yum!

SERVES 4–5

1¾ cups heavy cream

13½fl oz can coconut milk

¾ cup soft brown sugar

zest and juice of 2 limes

1½ envelopes (4½ teaspoons) unflavored gelatin

4–5 canned pineapple slices, drained

generous 1 tablespoon unsalted butter, plus extra for greasing molds

salt

Grease four or five small glasses or dariole molds.

In a small saucepan, heat the cream and coconut milk with ½ cup of the sugar, a pinch of salt, the lime zest, and half the lime juice. Heat, stirring often, until the sugar has dissolved. Remove from the heat, add the gelatin to the cream mixture, return to the heat, and cook for 1 minute, stirring constantly until fully dissolved.

Pour the mixture into the glasses, and put in the fridge to set for at least 4 hours.

When you're ready to serve, sprinkle the remaining ¼ cup of sugar over the pineapple slices. Warm a large, nonstick frying pan over medium heat, add the butter, then the pineapple, and cook on both sides until the pineapple is golden and sticky. Transfer to a plate, and squeeze over the remaining lime juice.

To turn out the coconut panna cottas, dip the glasses or molds into hot water briefly, and then invert each onto a plate. Serve each with a slice of caramelized pineapple.

CHOCOLATE & CHERRY POTS

Dark, rich, and decadent, these little pots are the perfect prep-ahead dessert.

SERVES 4

15oz can pitted cherries in syrup, roughly chopped and syrup reserved

juice of 1 lemon

2 tablespoons soft light brown sugar

2 egg yolks

5½oz dark chocolate, cut into small pieces

5½oz heavy cream

2 cardamom pods, bashed

salt

In a small frying pan, heat the cherries, syrup, lemon juice, and half the sugar until thickened. Divide the cherries between four glasses and refrigerate until needed.

Put the egg yolks and remaining sugar in a bowl with a pinch of salt. Whisk until pale, and increased in volume, and then set aside. Put the chocolate into a heatproof bowl and set aside.

In a small saucepan, heat the cream with the cardamom pods, stirring until it just comes to a boil.

Pour the hot cream through a strainer over the chopped chocolate. Leave to stand for 1 minute (to allow the chocolate to melt), then stir vigorously to amalgamate (it should come together and be glossy). Immediately pour the chocolate mixture over the egg yolk mixture, whisking constantly until combined.

Spoon the chocolate mixture over the cherry layer in the glasses, allow to cool, then refrigerate for at least 2 hours or until it's time to eat.

PINEAPPLE, LIME, & COCONUT CAKE

This upside-down cake has lost its maraschino cherries and gained the duo of coconut and lime. It's perfect served with a big scoop of rum raisin ice cream.

SERVES 10

For the pineapple layer

½ cup superfine sugar

scant 3 tablespoons unsalted butter

16oz canned pineapple rings in juice, drained

FOR THE SPONGE CAKE

7oz (1¾ sticks) unsalted butter, softened, plus extra for greasing

1 cup soft light brown sugar, plus 1 tablespoon

4 eggs

zest and juice of 2 limes

1½ cups self-rising flour

²/₃ cup dried shredded coconut

ice cream or cream, to serve

Preheat your oven to 325°F. Grease a 9-inch square cake pan (not loose-bottomed) with butter.

For the pineapple layer, Put the superfine sugar, along with 2 tablespoons of water, in a small saucepan over low heat to dissolve the sugar. Bring to a boil, and cook (without stirring) until it has turned a deep caramel color. Add the butter, and swirl to incorporate. Pour into the prepared cake pan to create an even layer on the base, then set aside to cool for a few minutes. Place the pineapple rings on top.

To make the sponge cake, beat the butter and 1 cup sugar together until light and fluffy. Beat in the eggs, one at a time, followed by the lime zest, then fold in the flour and coconut. Carefully spoon the mixture over the pineapple, and spread out so it's even. Bake in the oven for 35 minutes, until risen and golden. Meanwhile, mix the lime juice with the extra sugar and 1 tablespoon of water. Set aside.

Once the cake comes out, leave it to stand for 5 minutes, then turn out onto a plate and drizzle over the lime juice mixture; enjoy warm with a scoop of ice cream.

SPICED PUMPKIN & CHOCOLATE BREAD

A delicious and easy recipe that uses canned pumpkin, perfect for breakfast or teatime. Add a simple cream cheese icing, scattered with extra chopped pecans to turn it into more of a showstopper.

SERVES 8–10

9oz (1¹/₈ sticks) softened unsalted butter, plus extra for greasing

scant 1 cup superfine sugar

2 eggs

½ teaspoon vanilla extract

1⁷/₈ cups self-raising flour (white, whole-wheat or half and half)

½ teaspoon ground nutmeg

1 teaspoon ground cinnamon

1 heaping cup canned pumpkin purée

3oz dark chocolate, chopped

¾ cup chopped pecans, (or another nut of your choosing or dried fruit)

salt

Preheat your oven to 325°F. Grease a 9 x 5 x 3-inch loaf pan with butter, and line with parchment paper.

In a bowl, beat the butter and sugar together until pale and fluffy. Beat in the eggs, one at a time, then the vanilla. Fold in the flour, spices, a pinch of salt, and the pumpkin purée, followed by the chopped chocolate and pecans.

Pour into the prepared pan, and bake for about 60–70 minutes, until a toothpick poked into the center comes out clean. Leave to cool in the pan before turning out and diving in!

Tip: The spices can be changed or some left out; try using ground pumpkin pie spice, cloves, baharat mix, ginger, or orange zest.

CHERRY PIE

It is really worth making your own crust. Buttery and melt-in-the-mouth, it isn't too tricky, and doesn't take long. Try it.

SERVES 8

FOR THE CRUST

5½oz (1stick + 3 tablespoons) cold butter, cut into small cubes

scant 2¼ cups all-purpose flour, plus extra for rolling

pinch of salt

4½ tablespoons confectioners' sugar

2 egg yolks, plus 1 egg, beaten, for brushing

FOR THE FILLING

2 × 15oz cans pitted cherries in syrup, drained

2 tablespoons cornstarch

zest and juice of 1 lemon

12oz jar cherry jam

ice cream or cream, to serve

You will need a roughly 9½-inch pie pan. To make the crust, rub the butter into the flour, salt, and confectioners' sugar until it resembles damp sand. Add the egg yolks and 1–2 tablespoons of ice water. Using the rounded side of a butter knife, cut into the mixture until it starts coming together. When it starts to form large clumps, bring together into a ball with your hands. Flatten into a disc, wrap in plastic wrap, and chill in the fridge for 30 minutes (to ensure it's well chilled before you start rolling).

Meanwhile, to make the filling, combine all the ingredients in a large bowl.

Preheat the oven to 350°F, and pop a baking sheet in the oven to heat up while you build your pie. Remove your crust dough from the fridge, and cut off two thirds. Lightly dust the work surface with flour. Roll this into a circle slightly larger than your pie pan, lower into the pan, and gently press into the base and up the sides. Leave any overhang and brush the lip with a little of the beaten egg.

Roll the remaining dough into another circle large enough to form the lid. Spoon the filling into the pan, then press your second circle onto the egg-brushed overhang, squeezing together. Trim the two layers of dough using scissors about ³/₈ inch away from the edge of your pan, then crimp (you'll find lots of help on YouTube). Brush the top with the beaten egg, and poke a couple of holes into the lid.

Put the pie in the oven on the hot baking sheet, and bake for 30–40 minutes until golden. Leave to cool for about 30 minutes in the pan, then serve with a scoop of ice cream or a dollop of cream.

PEACH, MANGO, & PASSION FRUIT PAVLOVA

This impressive dessert, given a little time and care, isn't too tricky to pull off. I like to make it a day ahead, and leave it cooling in my oven overnight, ready to be finished the next day. If you're new to meringues, I urge you to give this a go.

SERVES 6–8

5 egg whites (very carefully separated to avoid any yolk contamination)

1¾ cups superfine sugar

1½ teaspoons cornstarch

1½ teaspoons white wine vinegar

zest of 2 limes and juice of 1 lime

15oz can peach slices, drained

15½oz can mango slices, drained

9fl oz (1 generous cup) heavy cream

7oz (1 scant cup) Greek yogurt

4 passion fruits, seeds scraped out

salt

Tips: Try crushing cardamom seeds, and adding them to the peach and mango mixture. Save all the egg yolks in the fridge for an extra indulgent omelet, or scrambled egg weekend breakfast.

Preheat the oven to 200°F, and line a large baking sheet with parchment paper. Draw a circle on the paper using a plate about 9 inches in diameter, then flip the paper so the marking is on the underside.

In a large bowl, slowly whisk the egg whites with a pinch of salt using an electric beater on medium speed, until peaks start forming. Gradually, 1 tablespoon at a time, beat in the sugar (ensuring it is fully incorporated and dissolved before adding more). Continue whisking until the mixture is stiff and glossy, and there is little to no graininess remaining. Mix the cornstarch and vinegar together, then fold in until just combined.

Scoop the meringue mixture onto the lined sheet and spread out to form a large circle, building the sides up a little so they are higher than the middle. Put into the oven, and bake for 1 hour, then turn the oven off, leaving the meringue inside to cool completely.

While you wait, put the lime zest and juice in a bowl with the peach and mango slices and a little pinch of salt.

When you're ready to assemble, whip the cream to soft peaks, fold in the yogurt, and carefully dollop over the top of the cooled meringue. Adorn with the peach mixture and passion fruit seeds. Serve immediately.

CREATIVE
CUPBOARD
ACCOMPANIMENTS

QUICK CHAPATIS

These are the easiest form of bread I've come across (except possibly going to buy some). Give them a go; they take minutes to make and only need four ingredients.

MAKES 4 (ABOUT THE SIZE OF A SIDE PLATE)

1½ cups whole-wheat or all-purpose white flour (or ideally half and half)

1½ tablespoons flavorless oil (such as sunflower)

1 teaspoon black onion seeds (optional)

salt

Tip: To make coconut roti, soak 1¹⁄3 cups of dried grated coconut in ²⁄3 cup boiling water for 10 minutes, add to 1½ cups all-purpose flour and 2 tablespoons melted butter, pinch of salt, and 1 teaspoon black onion seeds. Knead, rest, and cook as above.

In a large bowl, mix together the flour, a generous pinch of salt, the oil and the black onion seeds. Gradually add just enough warm water to make a soft, pliable dough; it should be about ½–²⁄3 cup. Knead for 5–10 minutes, until you have an elastic dough; the longer you knead, the softer it will be.

Place the dough back in the bowl and cover with a dish towel, then rest for at least 20 minutes.

When you're ready to cook the bread, divide the dough into four, and shape each into a ball (ensuring that you cover the dough you're not currently working on), then flatten the dough until it's the size of a side plate (about 8 inches). You can do this either by using a rolling pin or by pressing the dough in between your palms, working outwards, stretching occasionally.

Place a frying pan over high heat. Once it's really hot, add one chapati, and cook for about 30 seconds per side (there should be dark brown welts on each side, and it may puff up if your pan is really hot). Repeat the process with all four. Eat immediately.

COCONUT RICE

I could eat coconut rice on its own by the pan load; slightly sweet, yet salty, with a thoroughly savory note from the fenugreek.

SERVES 4

2¼ cups basmati rice

1 tablespoon flavorless oil (such as sunflower)

1 onion, minced

2 garlic cloves, sliced

1 teaspoon fenugreek seeds

14oz can coconut milk

salt

Wash the rice until the water runs clear, then put it in a bowl, and cover with cold water. Set aside for 30 minutes.

Meanwhile, heat the oil in a medium-sized, lidded saucepan, then add the onion, garlic, and fenugreek seeds. Sweat for 10 minutes over medium-low heat, until the onion is soft and sticky.

Once the rice has soaked, drain, and stir into the onion mixture along with a pinch of salt, the coconut milk, and 1½ cups of water. Bring to a boil, then cover, and immediately turn the heat to low. Cook for 7 minutes, turn off the heat, and set aside for 5 minutes, then take the lid off, and fluff up the rice using a fork. It's great served with the Tomato, Chickpea, & Okra Masala on page 66, or the Crab Thoran on page 79.

Tip: Try adding about 10–12 curry leaves along with the fenugreek seeds.

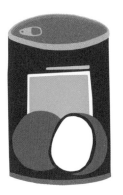

OATY SODA BREAD

This bread is sweet, salty, and rich. It's best eaten the same day it's made, but is still yummy toasted and slathered in butter for a few days after. If you can't get buttermilk, this can be made using plain yogurt.

MAKES 1 LOAF

scant 1¼ cups all-purpose flour

scant 1¼ cups whole-wheat flour

1 teaspoon fine salt

1½ teaspoons baking soda

½ cup rolled oats

1 teaspoon sugar

1¼ cups buttermilk

2½ tablespoons molasses

Tips:
If you can't get through a whole loaf, slice it up and freeze so you have it ready to go straight into the toaster.

Try adding a handful of sultanas or raisins, and some roughly chopped walnuts to the dry ingredients.

Preheat the oven to 350°F. Mix together all the dry ingredients in a large bowl.

Once the oven has reached temperature, make a well in the center of your dry mixture, and pour in the buttermilk and molasses. Using a wooden spoon, mix until you have a soft, sticky dough.

Using floured hands, shape the dough into a round, then pop onto a lightly floured baking sheet. Using a sharp knife, cut a deep cross about one-third of the way through the dough, and dust with flour. Bake for 45–50 minutes, until the loaf sounds hollow when tapped underneath.

Leave to cool on a wire rack before eating. Try spreading with the molasses butter overleaf for a decadent snack.

MOLASSES BUTTER

This was conceived midway through testing a cake recipe. The slightly savory and metallic molasses, with salty butter and a little sugar, makes for a splendid spread; try it on warm soda bread.

SERVES 4

¾ stick slightly salted butter, softened

2½ tablespoons soft light brown sugar

3 tablespoons molasses

Beat the butter with the sugar until really soft, then slowly beat in the molasses until well-combined. Eat slathered over warm Oaty Soda Bread (see page 148) or with Pear Pancakes (see page 114).

FLAKY PIE CRUST DOUGH

This buttery pie crust dough is perfect for tarts, pies, and quiches. If you don't need the whole amount, it can be easily frozen for a couple of months, then defrosted overnight in the fridge when you need it next.

MAKES ENOUGH TO LINE A 10-INCH TART PAN

1¹/₃ sticks very cold butter, diced

heaping 2 cups all-purpose flour

good pinch of salt

2 egg yolks

To make the pie crust dough, rub the butter into the flour and salt until it resembles damp sand. Add the egg yolks, and 1–2 tablespoons of very cold water. Using the rounded side of a butter knife, cut into the mixture until it starts coming together. When it starts to form large clumps, bring together into a ball with your hands. Flatten into a disc, wrap in plastic wrap, and chill in the fridge for 30 minutes before using.

MANGO CHUTNEY

To be honest, I was pretty astonished that mango chutney can be made (and made deliciously), from canned mango. Ditch the fluorescent orange chutney from the stores; this is worth making.

MAKES 1 JAR (ABOUT 1½ CUPS)

2 × 15oz cans mango slices in juice, drained, and chopped into small chunks

1 teaspoon red pepper flakes

1oz fresh ginger (about 1½-inch piece), peeled and grated

4 garlic cloves, minced

scant 1 cup soft light brown sugar

1 cup white wine or cider vinegar

1 teaspoon black onion seeds

Add everything to a saucepan, bring to a boil, then turn down to a simmer for about 40–50 minutes until thick and jammy, remembering to stir occasionally to check it's not catching on the bottom. Scoop into a hot, sterilized jar. Allow to cool slightly, then seal. Once open, store it in the fridge; it should keep for a few months.

Tip: Try popping a layer of this under some Cheddar for your next cheese on toast. It's the best.

FIG & RED ONION JAM

This is the perfect partner for cheese, ham, pâté, or cooked meats.

MAKES ABOUT 18FL OZ

3 tablespoons olive oil

18oz red onions, finely sliced

6 tablespoons soft brown sugar

14oz can figs, roughly chopped, syrup reserved

2 bay leaves

1 star anise

$^{2}/_{3}$ cup red wine vinegar

$^{1}/_{3}$ cup Marsala (or red wine)

salt and freshly ground black pepper

Heat the oil in a large frying pan over medium-low heat. Add the onions along with a pinch of salt, and fry gently for about 30 minutes until they are very soft.

Next, add 2 tablespoons of the sugar, with the figs, bay leaves, and star anise, then continue to cook for 10 minutes. Add the vinegar and Marsala (or red wine), and remaining sugar, then season. Bring to a boil, then turn down to a simmer for about 30–40 minutes, until the mixture becomes sticky and jam-like. Keep your eye on it, in case it sticks or dries out.

Scoop into a hot, sterilized jar. Allow to cool slightly, then seal. Once open, store it in the fridge; it should keep for a few months.

A KICK-ASS ANCHOVY DRESSING

This dressing is great for leafy salads, boiled potatoes, or green veggies (roasted, boiled, or steamed), or even tossed through pasta with a can of tuna thrown in. Easy-peasy dinners.

MAKES ABOUT ²/₃ CUP

1 shallot, minced

1 tablespoon vinegar (white wine or cider)

2oz can anchovy fillets, drained and finely chopped

1 teaspoon Dijon mustard

1 garlic clove, minced

½ teaspoon red pepper flakes

¹/₃ cup of your nicest olive oil

1 tablespoon chopped oregano, basil, or parsley (optional)

salt and freshly ground black pepper

In a bowl, mix the shallot and vinegar together, then set aside for 5 minutes.

Add the anchovies, mustard, garlic, and red pepper flakes to the shallot. Gradually beat in the olive oil, check and adjust the seasoning, and add any herbs, if using. It'll keep well in a sealed jar, or an airtight container in the fridge for about a week.

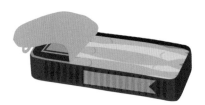

BREAD CRUMB TOPPING

A versatile, crunchy addition to many dishes. Great for adding some extra texture and a boost of flavor. Try experimenting with red pepper flakes, caraway, fennel, or cumin seeds, chopped nuts, or other citrus zest.

SERVES 4

2 tablespoons olive oil

1 garlic clove, minced

1¾ cups fresh bread crumbs (see Tip)

¼ cup blanched almonds, roughly chopped (optional)

zest of 1 lemon (optional)

In a frying pan, heat the oil with the garlic, bread crumbs (and almonds, if using). Fry for 5–10 minutes, stirring often until golden. Stir through the lemon zest, if using, and serve.

Tips:
To make 1¾ cups fresh bread crumbs, remove the crusts from about 2 thick slices of crusty bread and rub into large crumbs.

Keep any leftovers in a sealed container in the fridge for a few days; they won't be quite as crisp, but will still be delicious.

CORN & CHEESE MUFFIN LOAF

I am a lifelong corn fan. I always have a can in my rucksack for festivals or camping; it is best eaten straight out of the can, accompanied by a chunk of Cheddar cheese. Here these two meet in a loaf.

SERVES 8–10

¾ cup plain yogurt

2 eggs

¾ stick unsalted butter, melted and cooled

1½ cups canned whole kernel corn, drained

bunch of scallions, finely sliced

4 oz aged Cheddar cheese, grated (about 1¼ cups)

scant 2 cups self-rising flour

2 teaspoons hot paprika

1 teaspoon baking powder

Preheat the oven to 325°F, and line a 9 x 5 x 3-inch loaf pan with parchment paper.

In a jug, whisk together the yogurt, eggs, butter, corn, scallions, and two-thirds of the cheese, then season. In a large bowl, mix together the flour, paprika, and baking powder. Pour the jug contents into the bowl, stirring until combined.

Pour evenly into the prepared pan, sprinkle with the remaining cheese, and bake for 45–55 minutes until golden, well-risen, and a toothpick inserted into the center comes out clean. Leave to cool in the pan for 10 minutes, then put on a wire rack to cool further. Best eaten the same day warm or cold, but will keep in an airtight container for about 4 days.

INDEX

THANK YOU.

Jamie, thank you for supporting me and believing in me, and for always listening while I wittered on about all things canned for nearly a whole year! You're incredible and I feel very lucky to have you by my side.

Mom and dad, you've been there for everything. Thank you for your guidance, love, and your endless recipe testing and tasting. Brodie, thank you for being full of encouraging words wherever you are, and always being willing to be my guinea pig. Aunty Sarah, my creative council, I love bouncing ideas about with you over copious amounts of lentils and tea. Although you're not about to read this, Granny Susan, thank you for planting the cooking seed, for always cooking around me, feeding, and teaching me. You were such an amazing source of creativity and imagination. I'm sad I haven't been able to share this with you.

Thank you to Judith, for giving me the opportunity to write this book — it was something I had always dreamed of, but never thought would happen to me. Isabel, thank you for being such a wonderful and patient editor. Lizzie, thank you so much for your gorgeous pictures, and Louie for your beautiful props. Thank you Amélie for being a total gem. Steph, thank you, for all of your help. Louise, thank you bringing it all together with your brilliant design. We Are Out of Office, thank you for your marvelous illustrations, I love them.

To all of my freelance work family, thank you so much for encouraging and believing in me and being totally fabulous.

Carolyn, thank you for being so understanding and patient while I totally took over the kitchen every day for months. To all the wondrous people who have tested recipes along the way, thank you — Jaz, Rio, Esther, John, Alice, Faye, Sophie, Starzy, Ags, Rachel (also thank you for your amaze proofing), Lindsay, Eleanor, Emily, Sera, Tazi, and Rilwan. To all the tasters, thank you, too.

Lola's eyes were opened to the world of cookbooks, food photography, and styling when she did work experience with Jamie Oliver and his food team. After school, she went to Glasgow School of Art and studied Fine Art Photography, though food continued to weave through her work there. After graduating she decided to return to the world of food styling and started working in the kitchens of cafes and bakeries while doing work experience with food stylists. She then progressed to assisting full time and then to being a stylist herself, expanding along the way into recipe testing and then writing.